A Caboodle of Doodles

Volume I

Adult coloring book

Featuring the art of Renée Lawrence

No part of this book may be reproduced or transmitted by any form or by any means, electronic or mechanical, including photocopy, recording, or any information storage or retrieval system, without the prior written consent from the author.

© 2020 Renée Lawrence. All rights reserved.

For Vanessa, the best sister in the whole wide world!

THIS coloring book had its beginnings as a coronavirus pandemic project. In March 2020, the whole world was retreating or had already retreated to the safety of their homes, and so had I. As an artist, I wanted to do something creative as well as offer a fun distraction for my friends during these challenging times. So I started creating original coloring pages and sharing them on Facebook. That turned into a Facebook group, Coloring with Renée, and that turned into this coloring book.

It is now almost August 2020, and so many of us are still staying close to home. I hope this coloring book can be picked up by you — by anyone anywhere in the world — and that you too will find in it a fun distraction, a moment's forgetfulness, and a humble reminder that we are all creative beings.

We are all in this together. Be kind, be loving, be gentle ... and keep coloring.

Renée

P.S. The last two doodles in this book are a sneak preview of a future coloring book, but they are especially fitting for today.

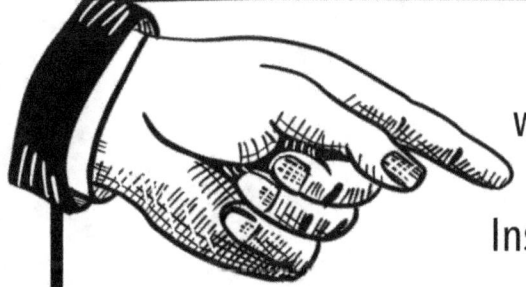

Website
www.reneelawrenceart.com
Instagram
Instagram.com/okie_doodling
Zazzle
www.zazzle.com/store/Universal_Wisdom?rf=238580446291150903
Fine Art America
fineartamerica.com/profiles/renee-lawrence
Facebook Coloring with Renee group
www.facebook.com/groups/205888947382187/
Amazon
Visit Renee's author page to see her other offerings

Check it out!

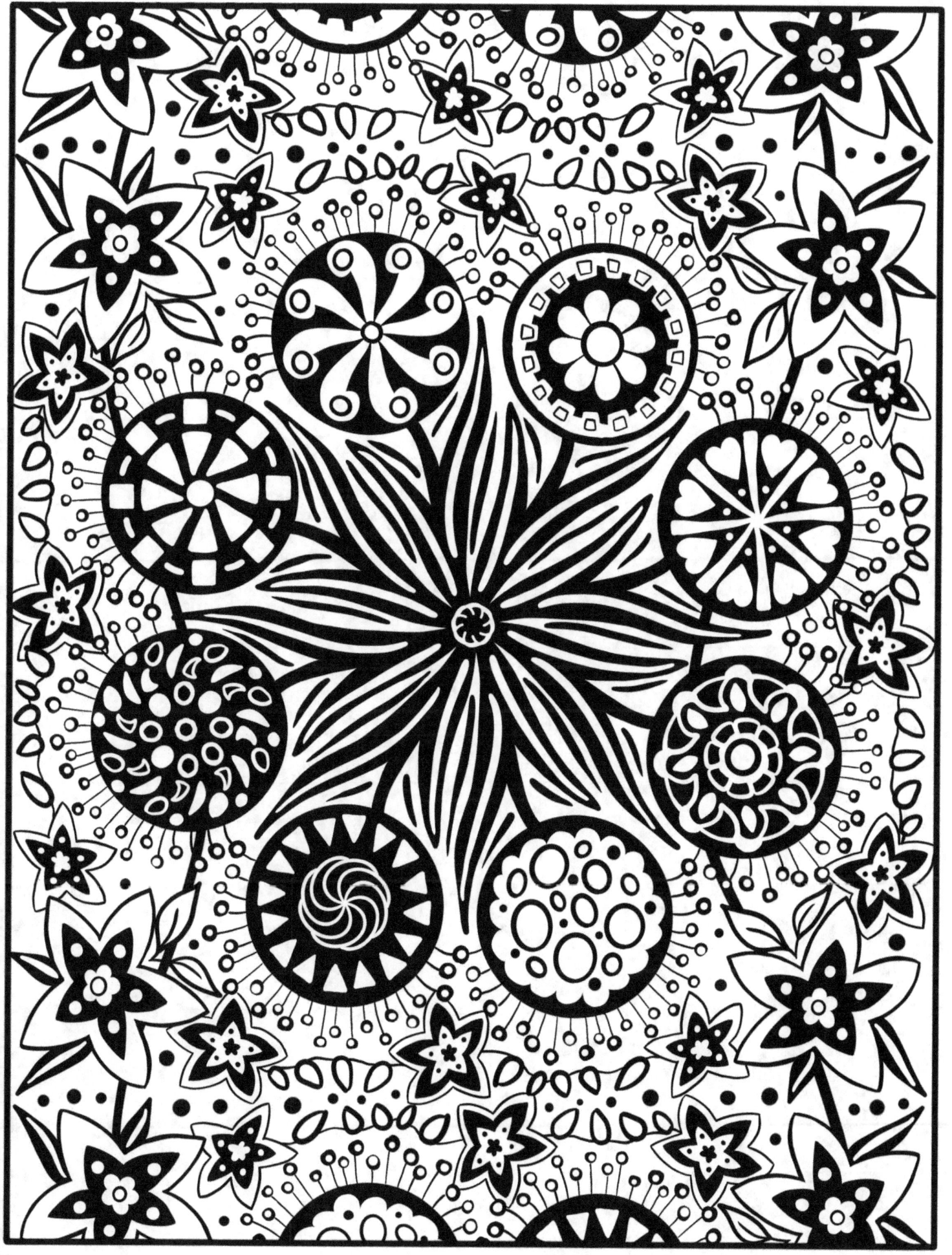

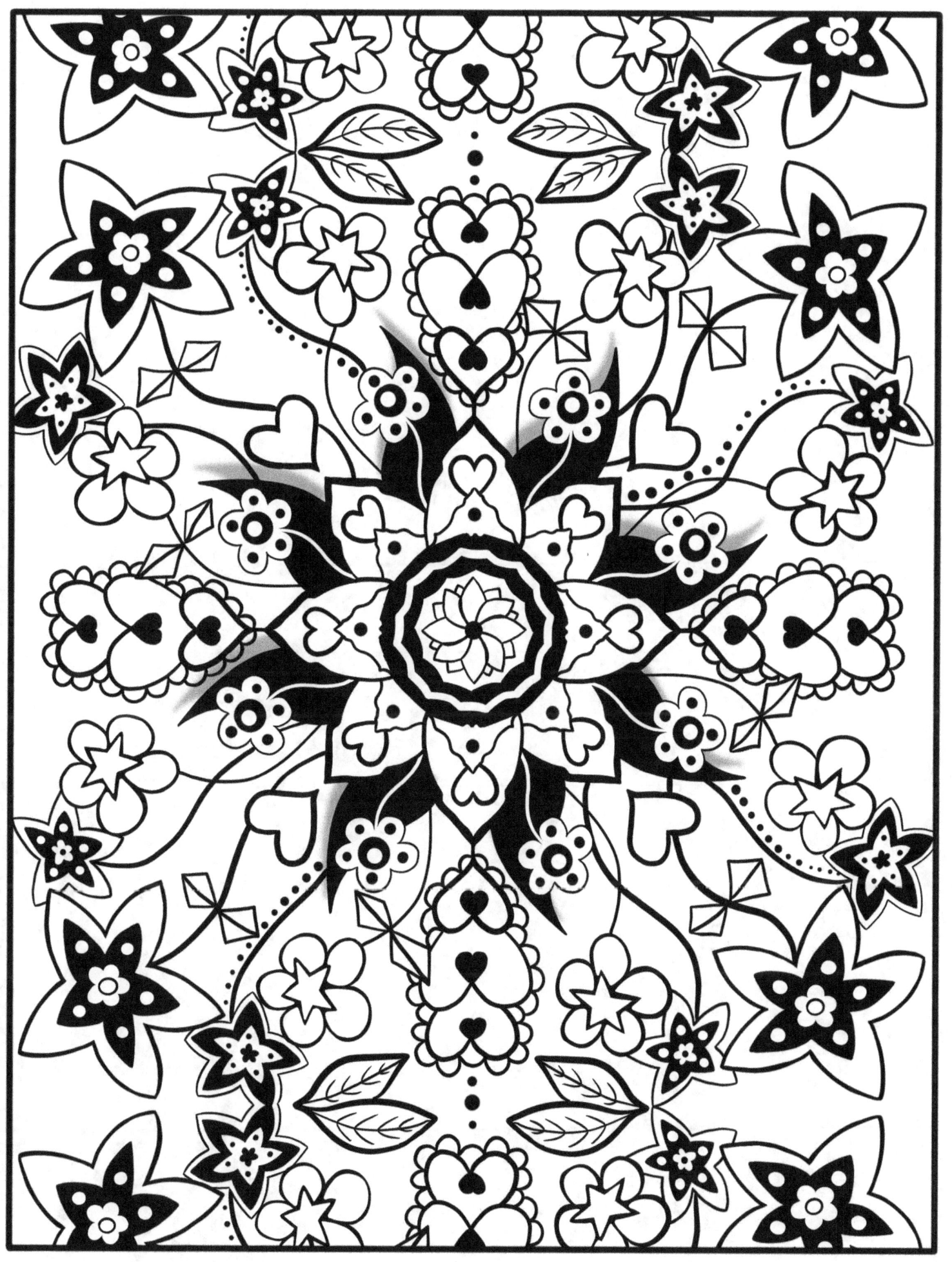

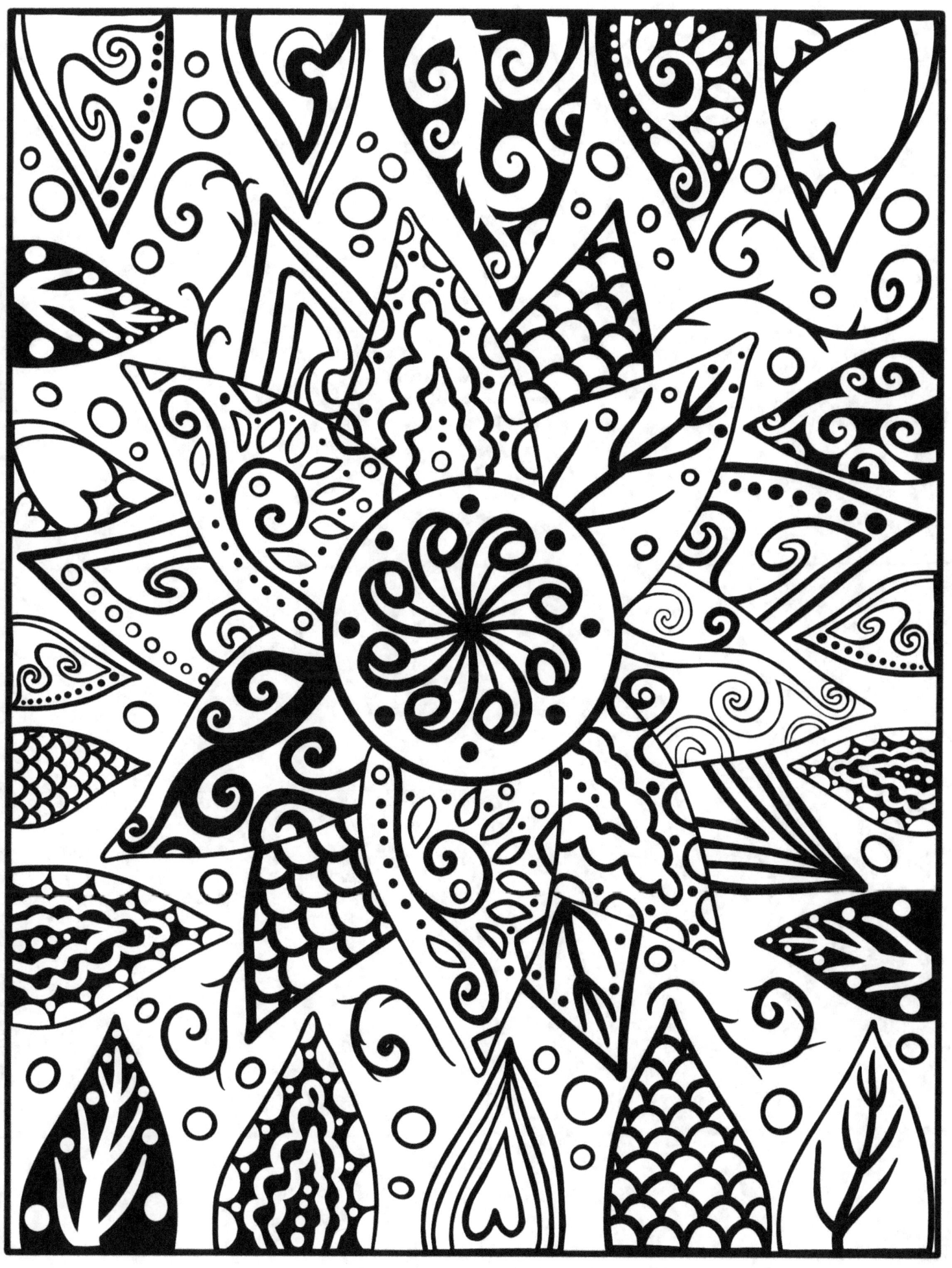

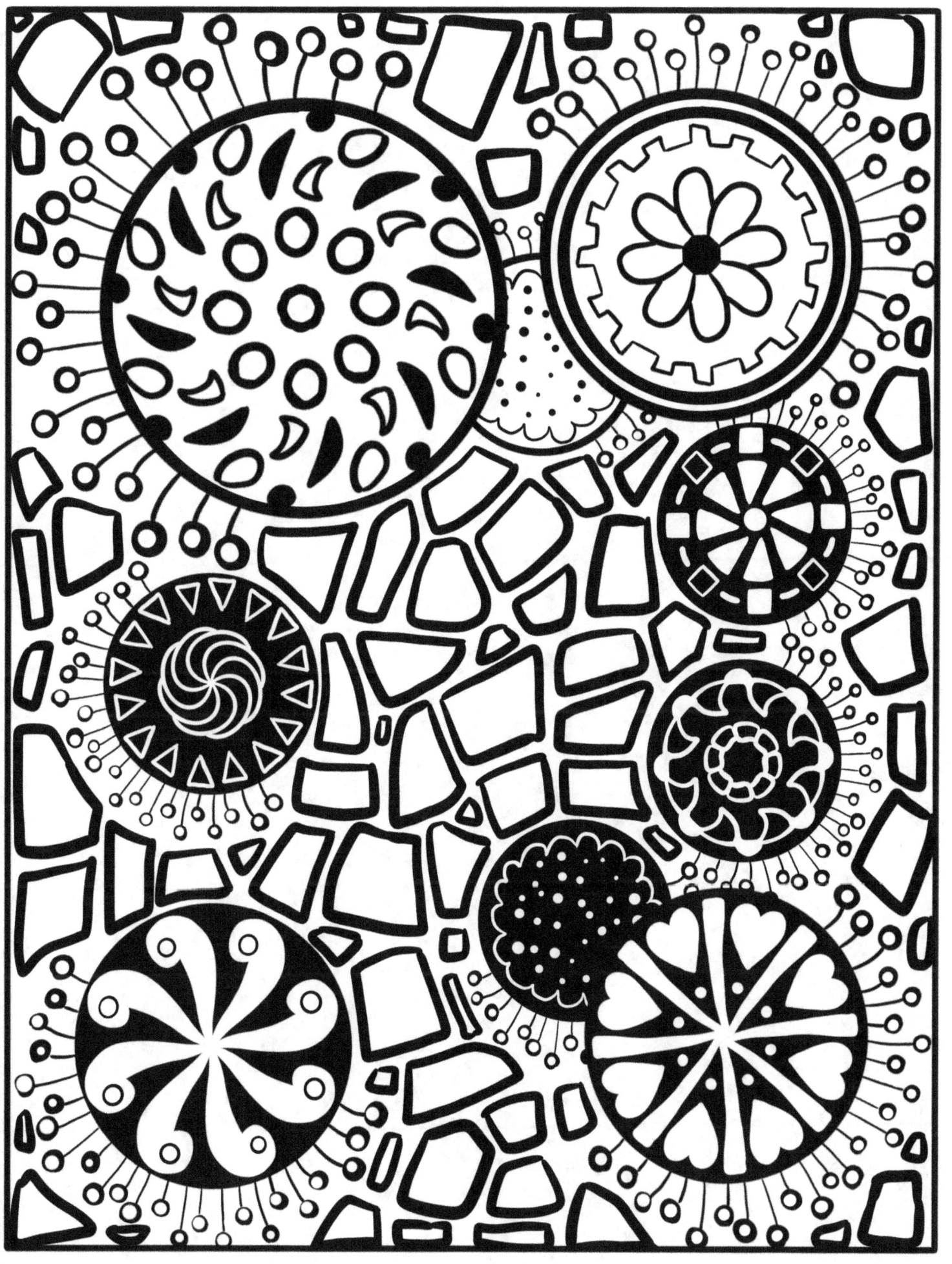

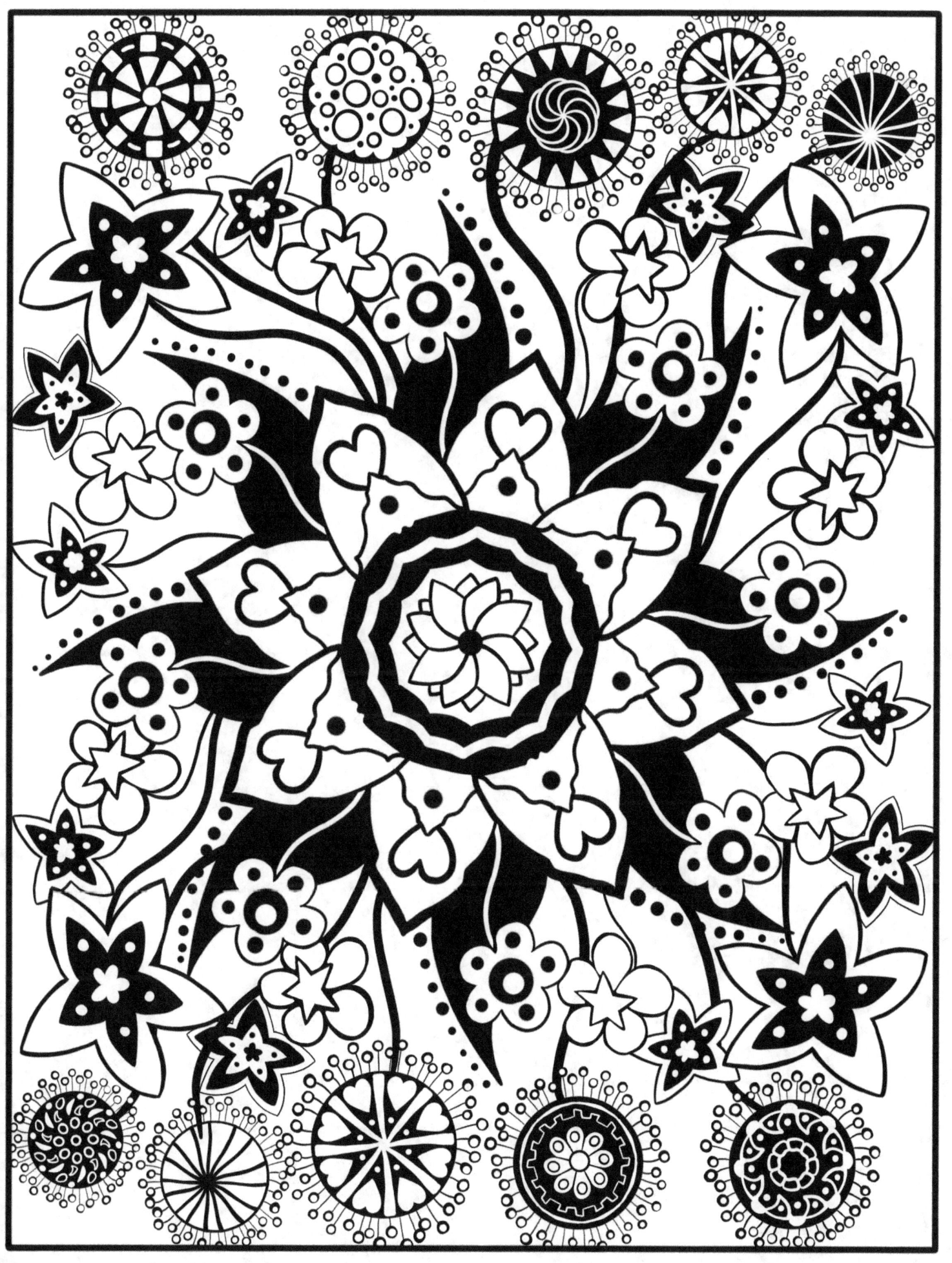

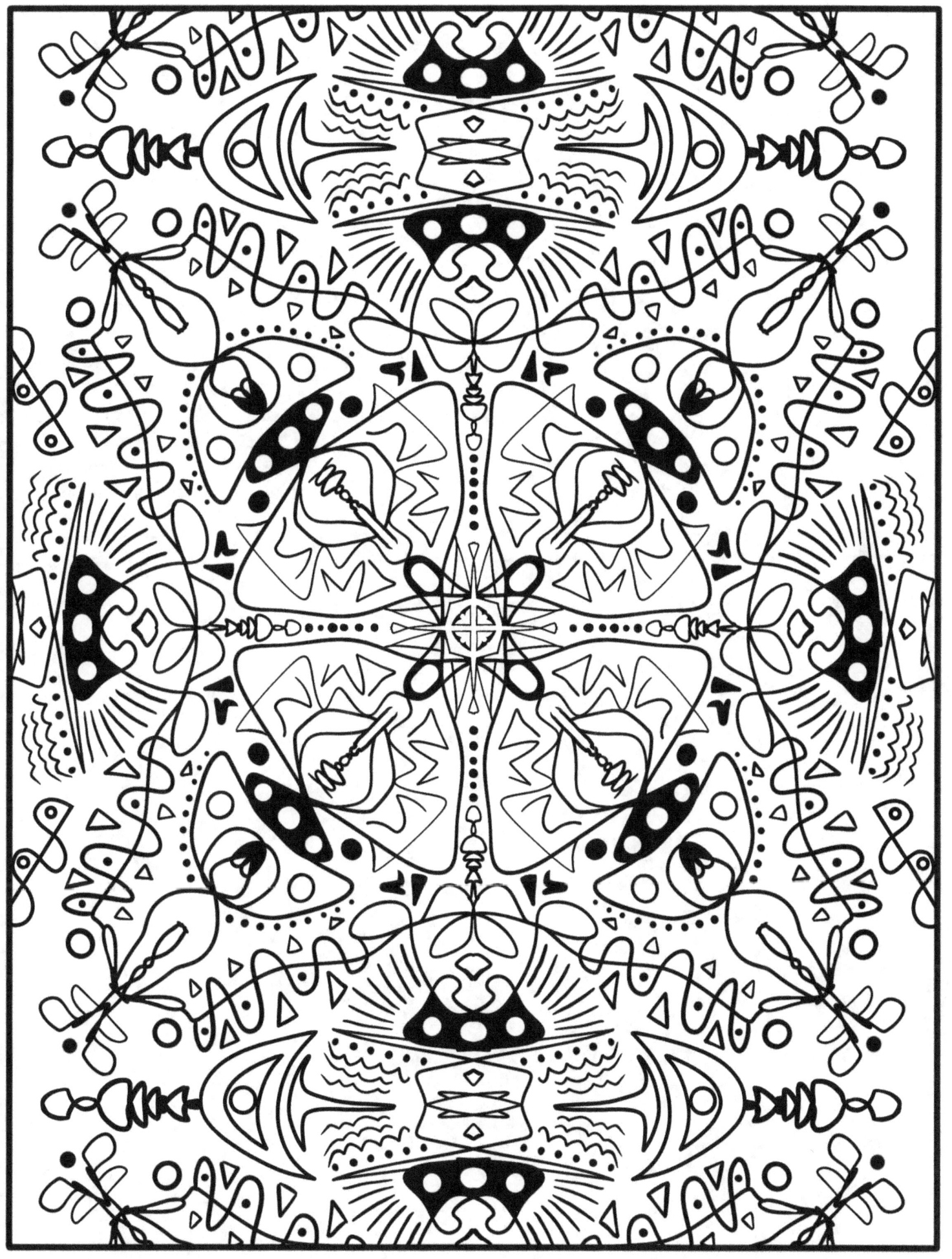

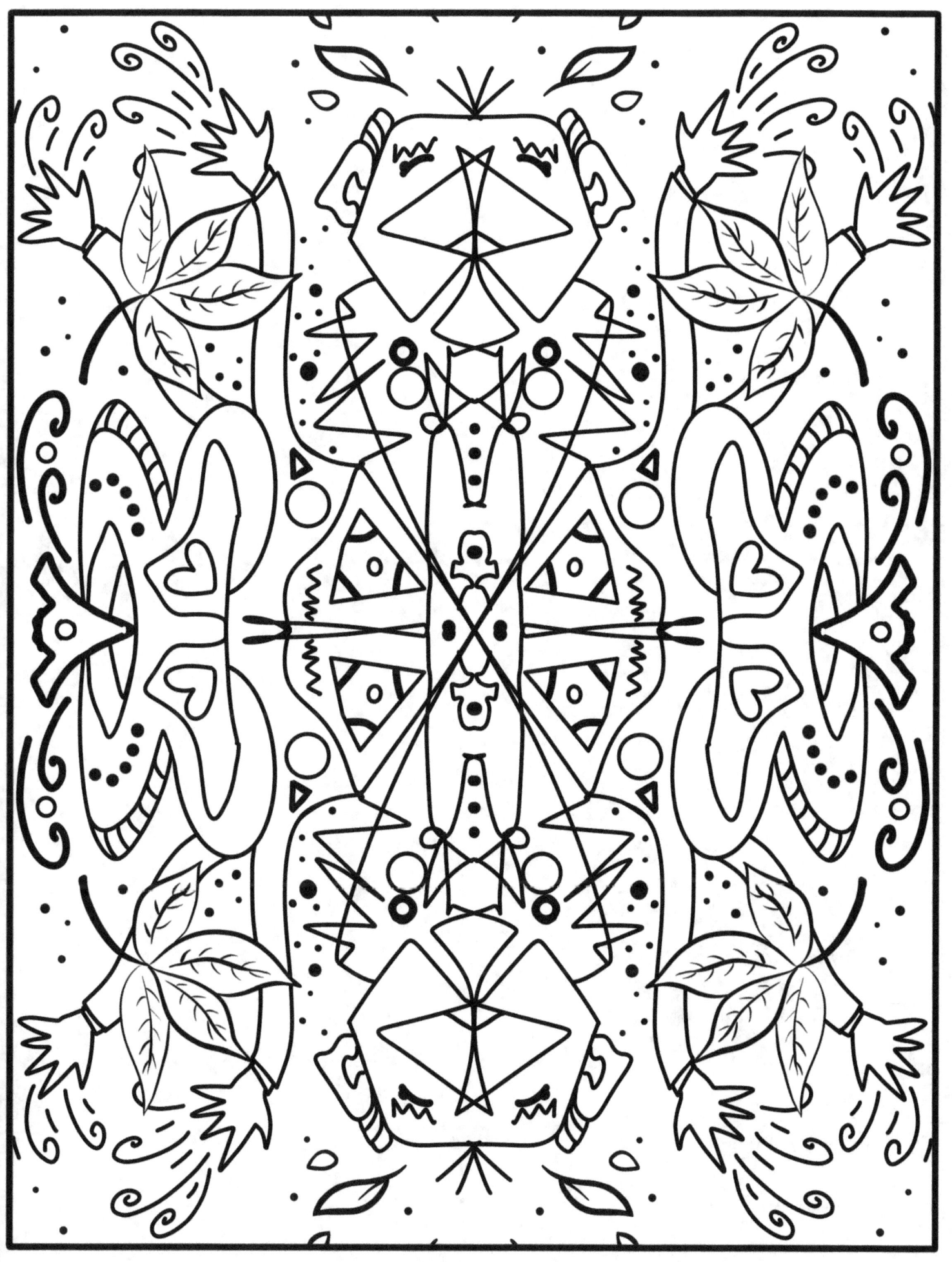

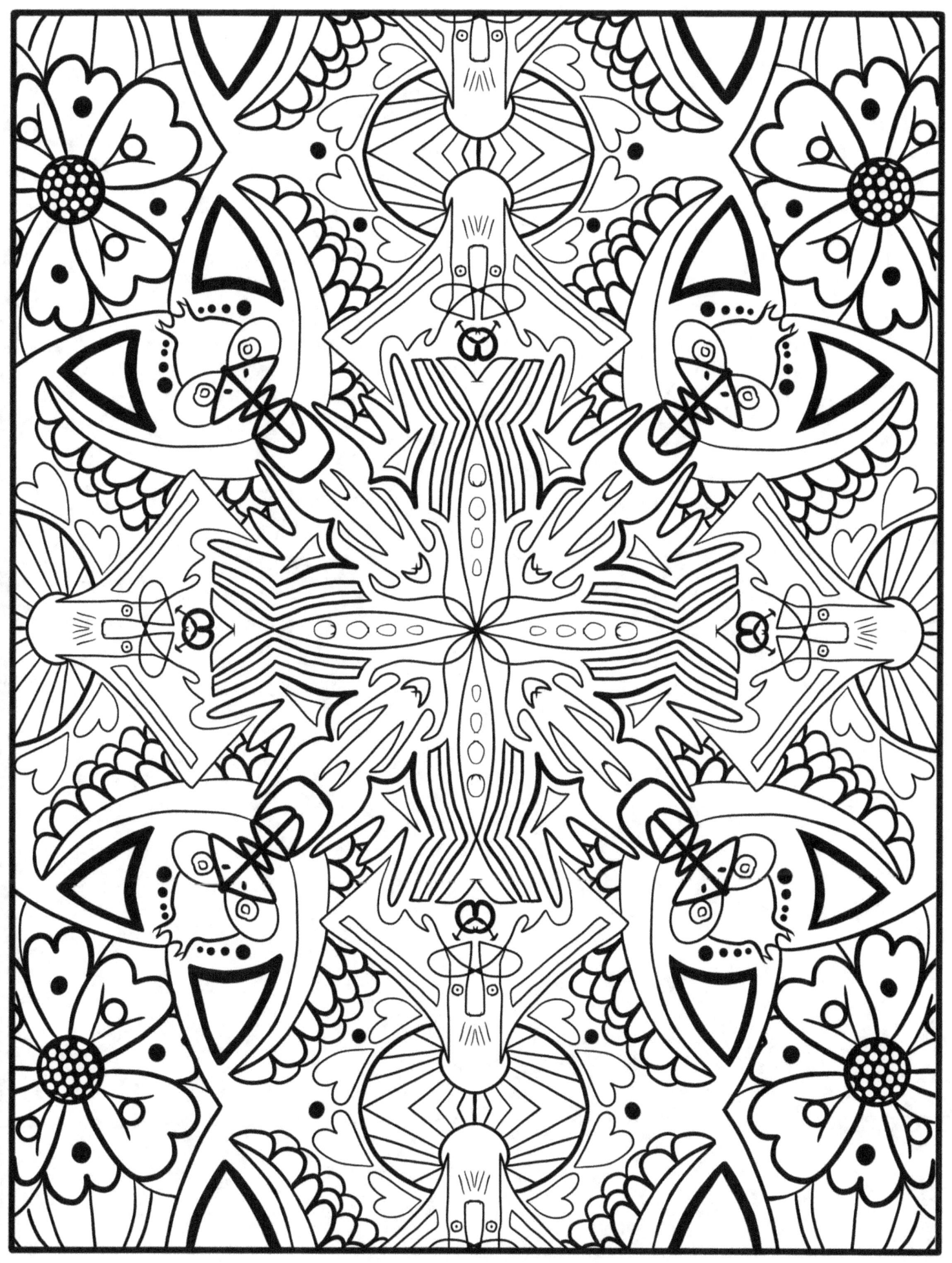

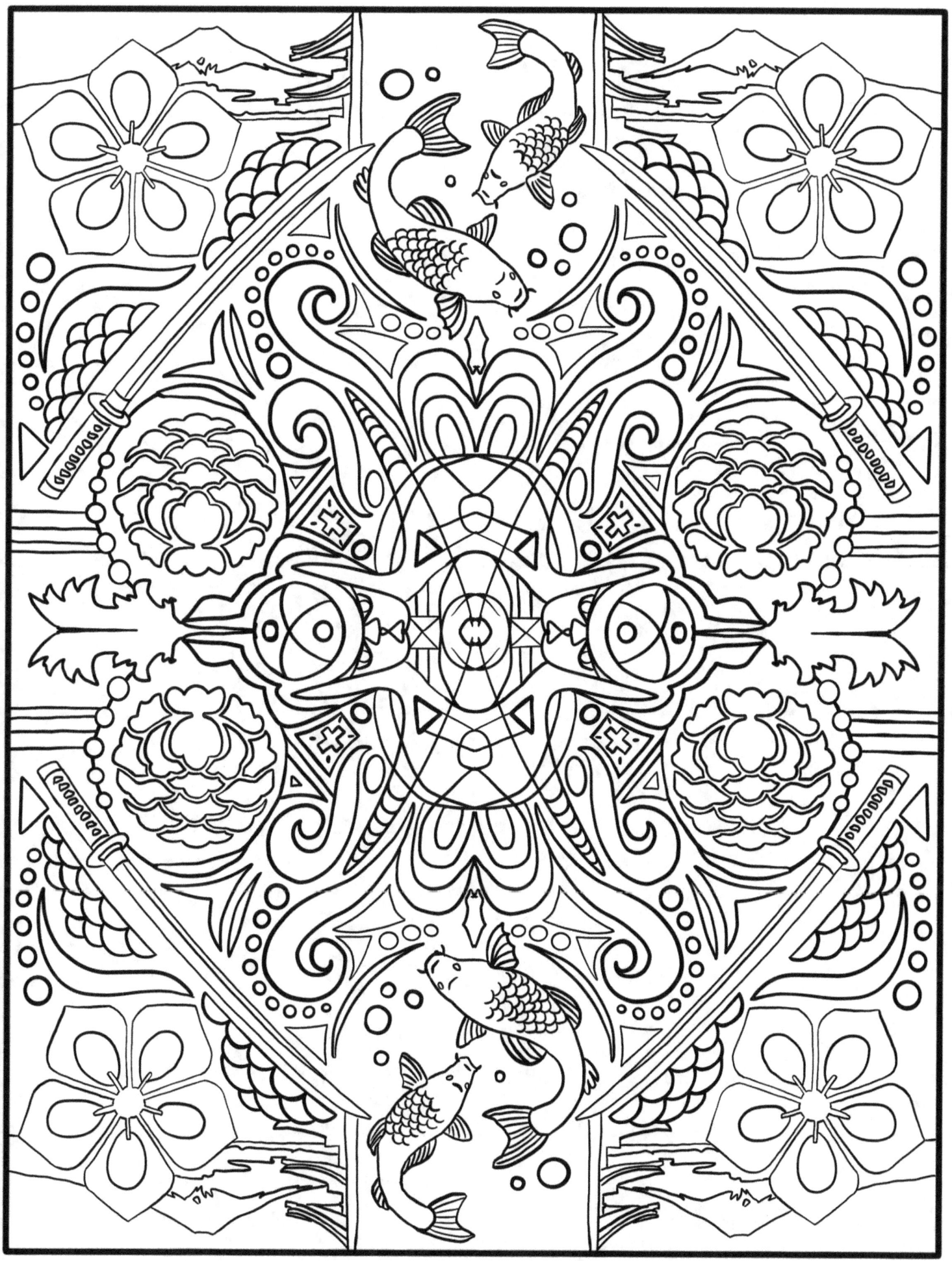

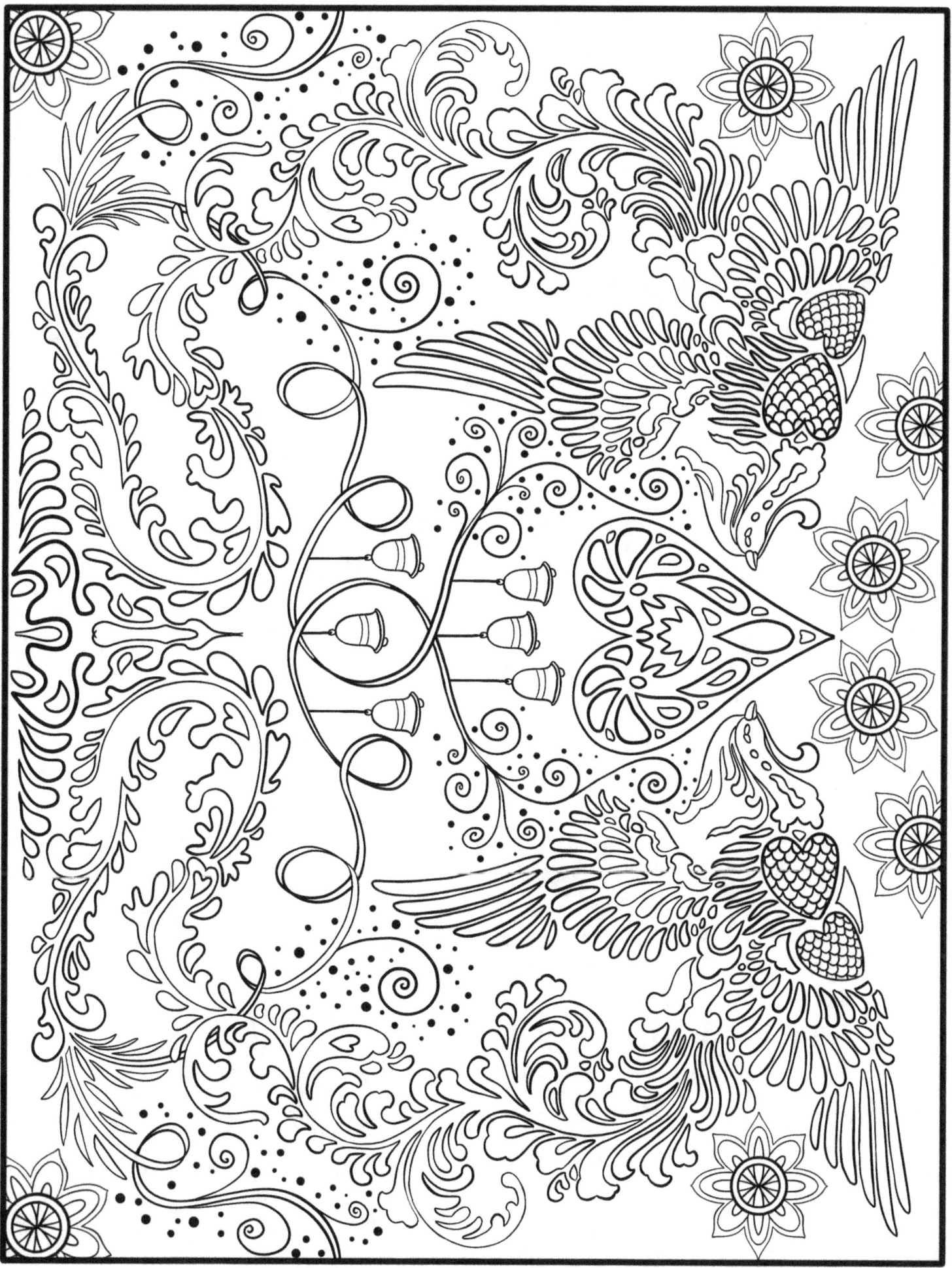

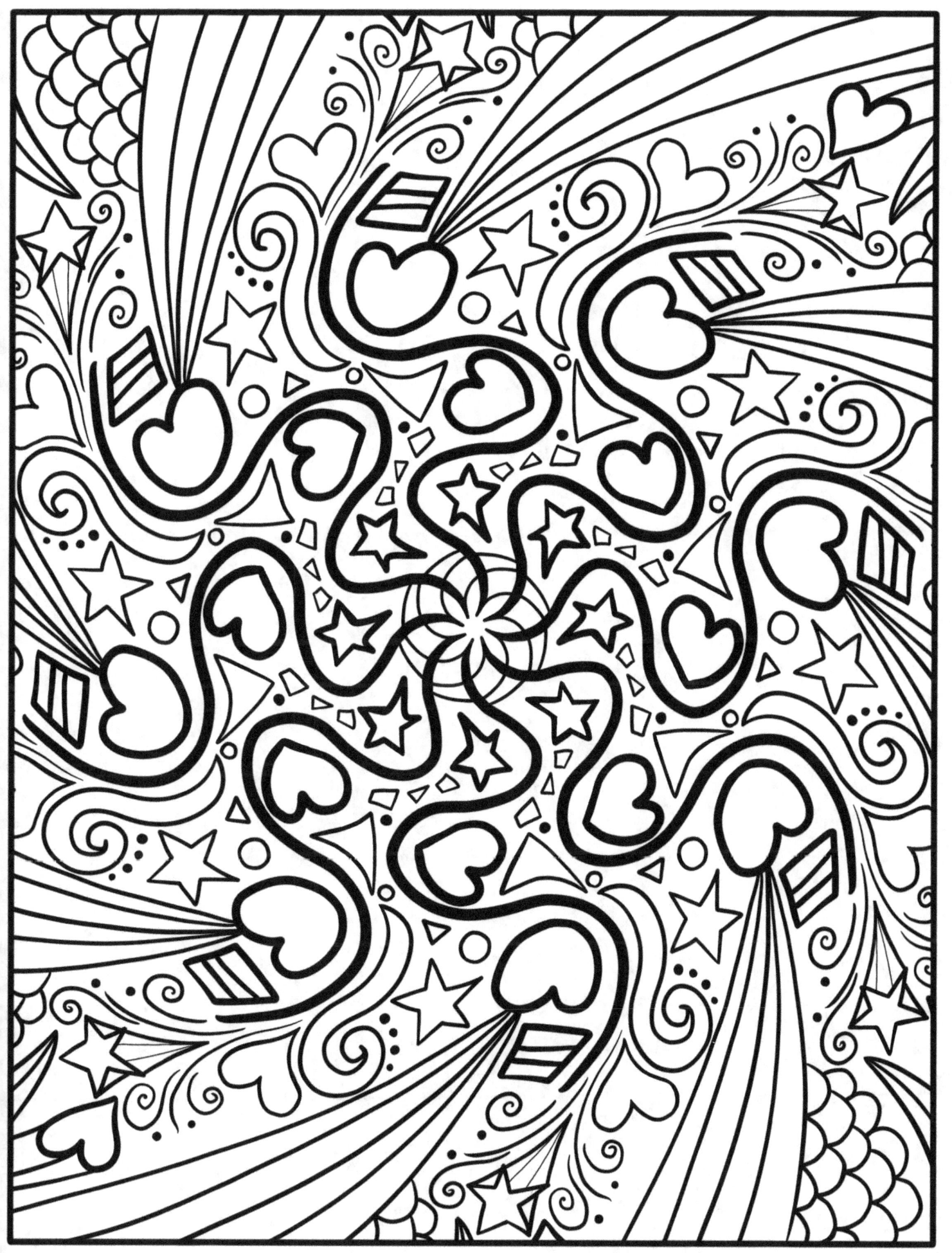

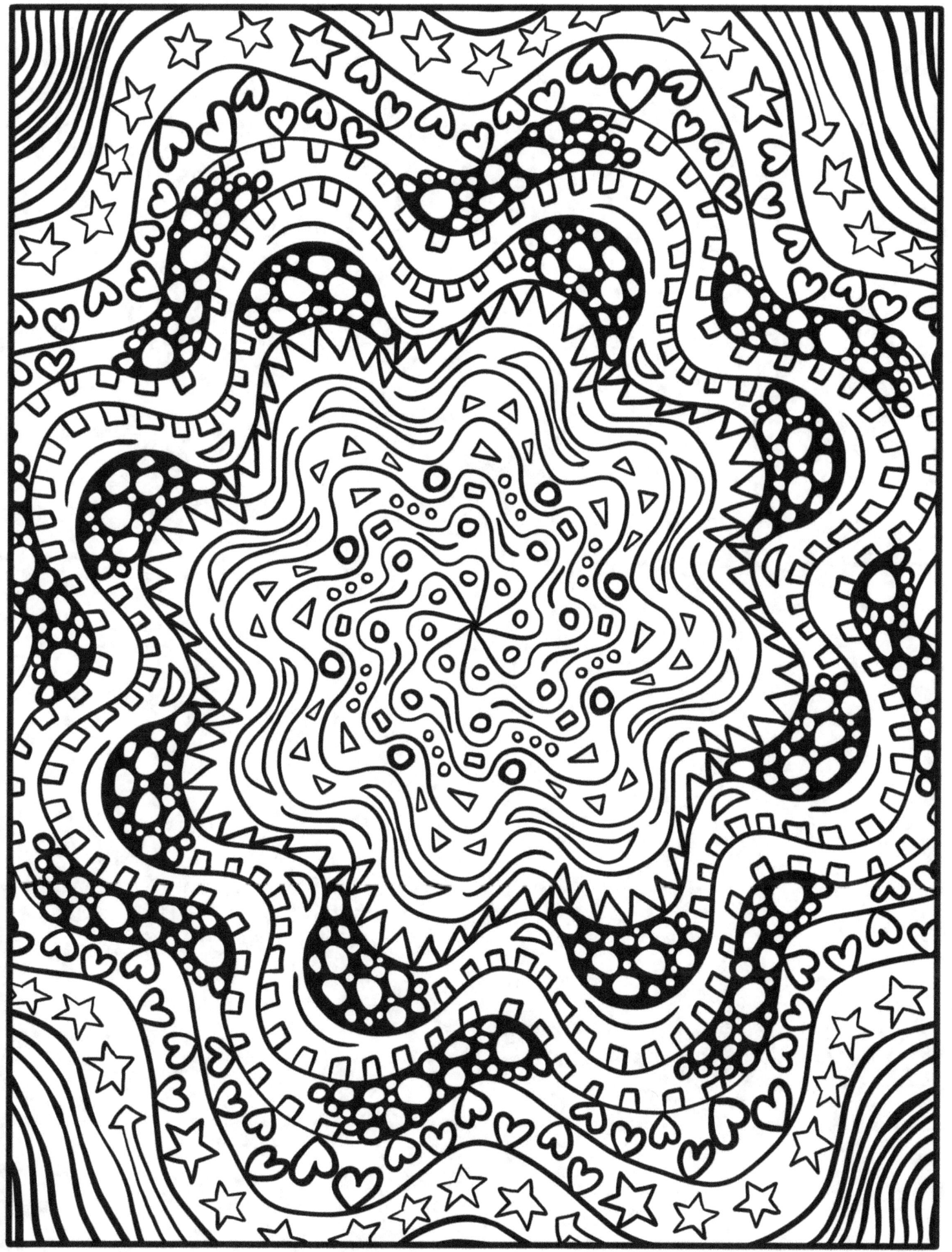

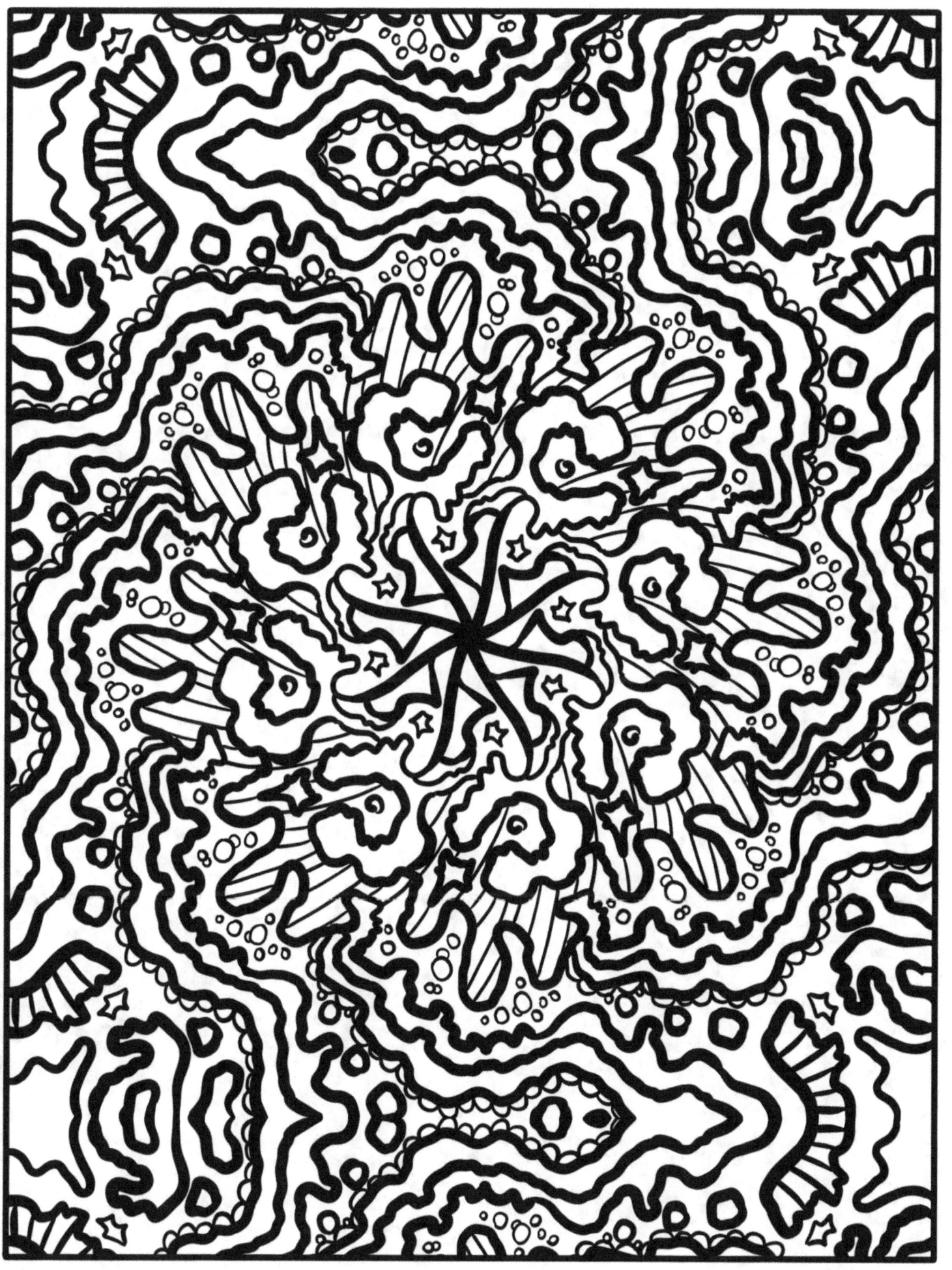

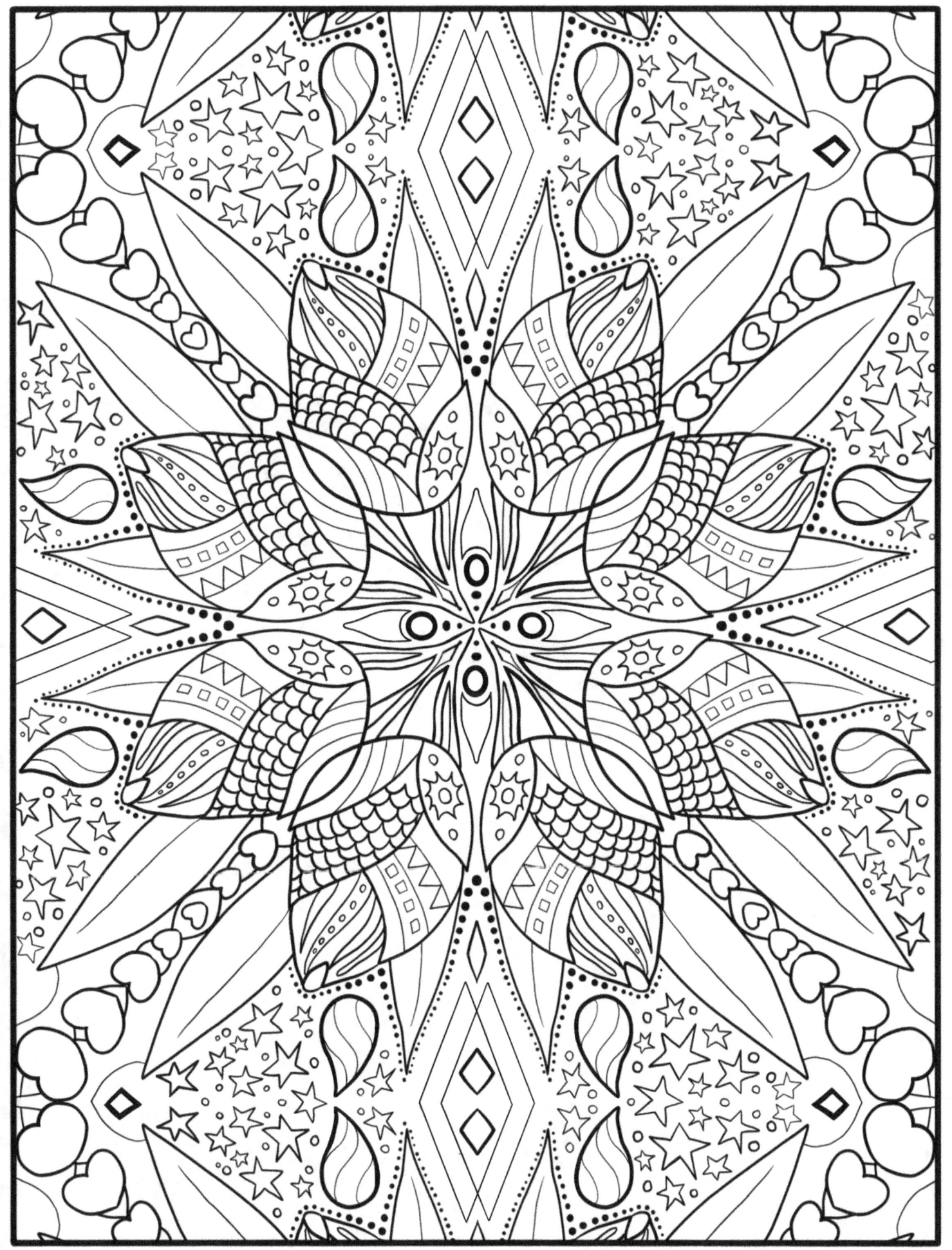

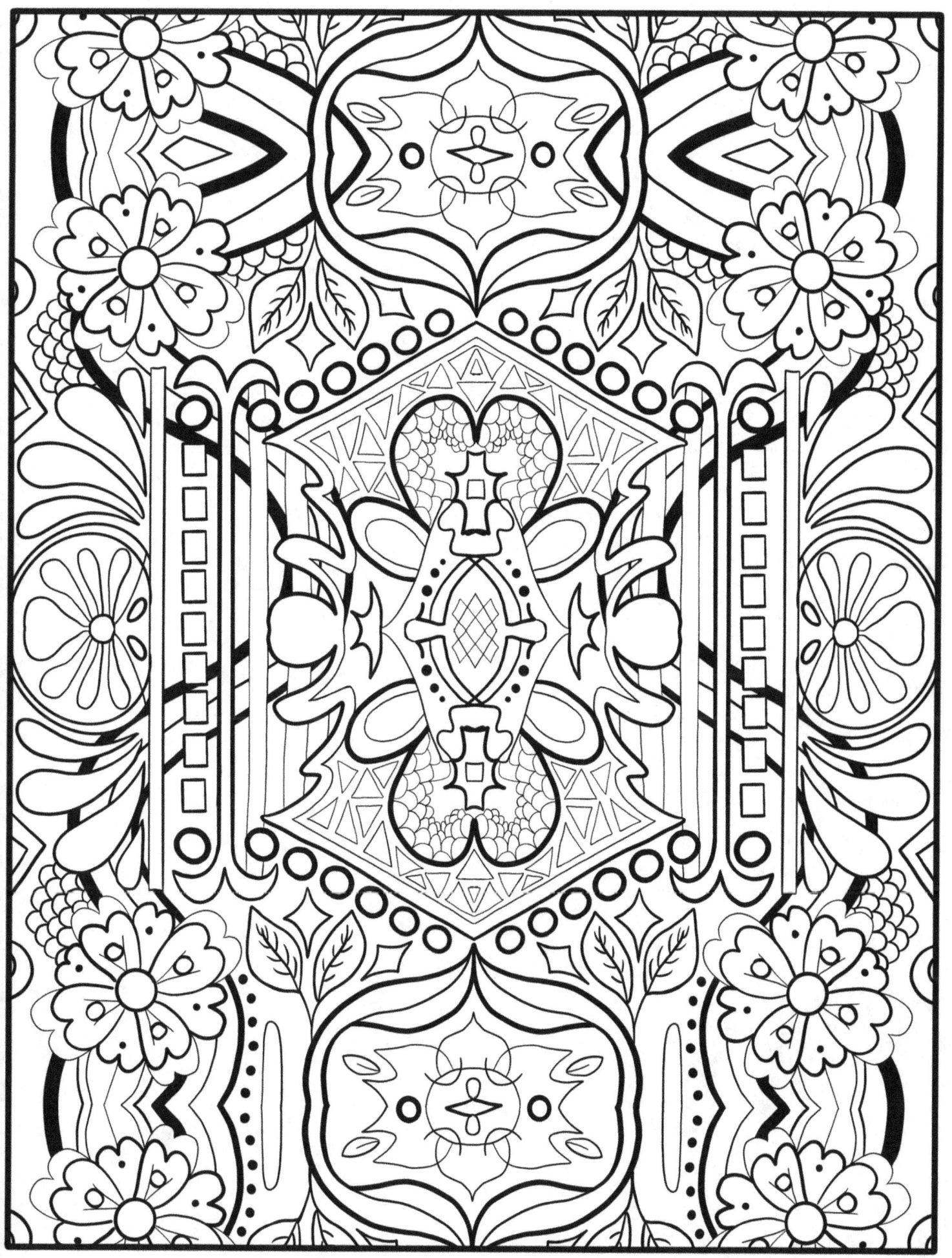

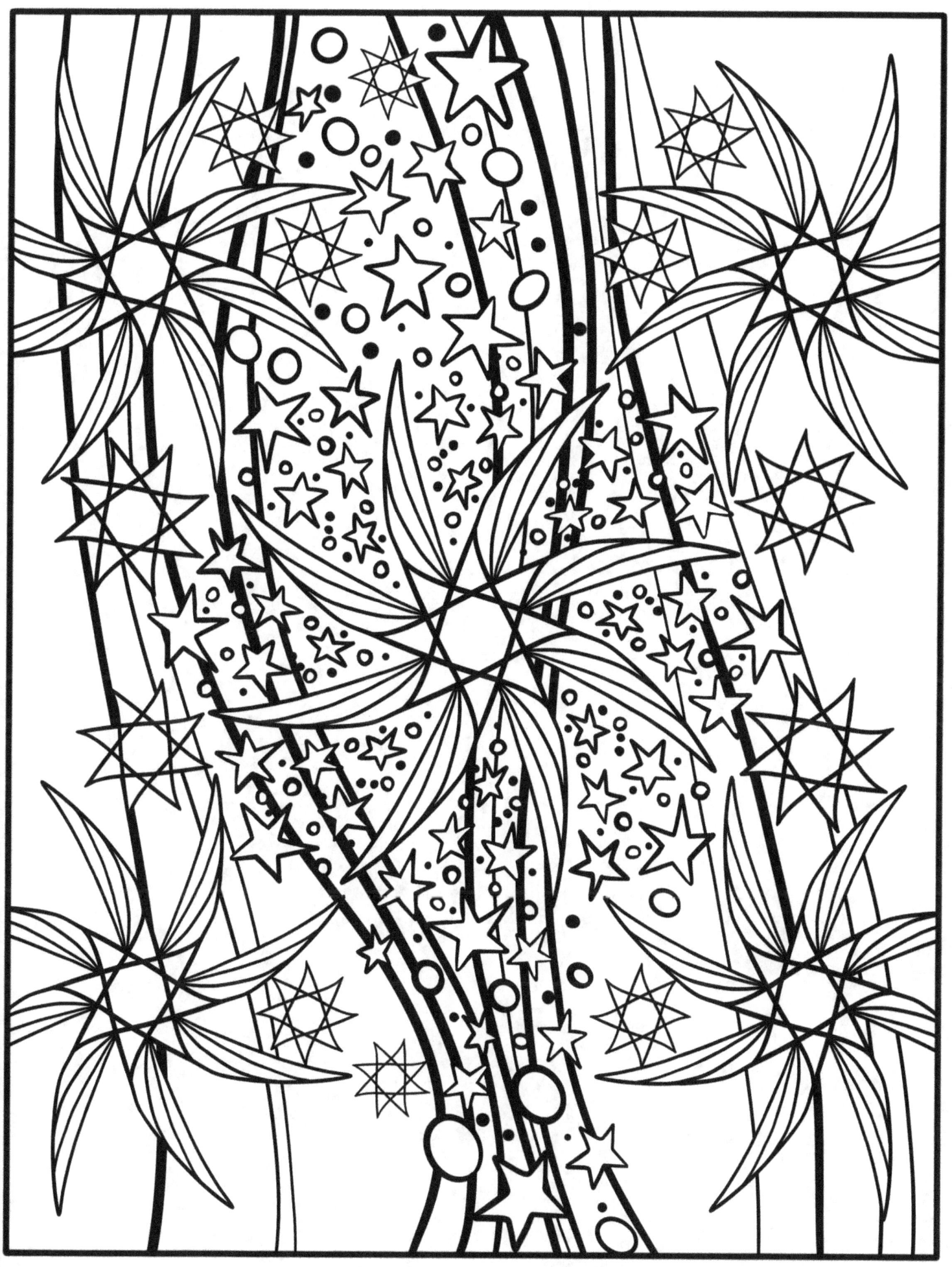

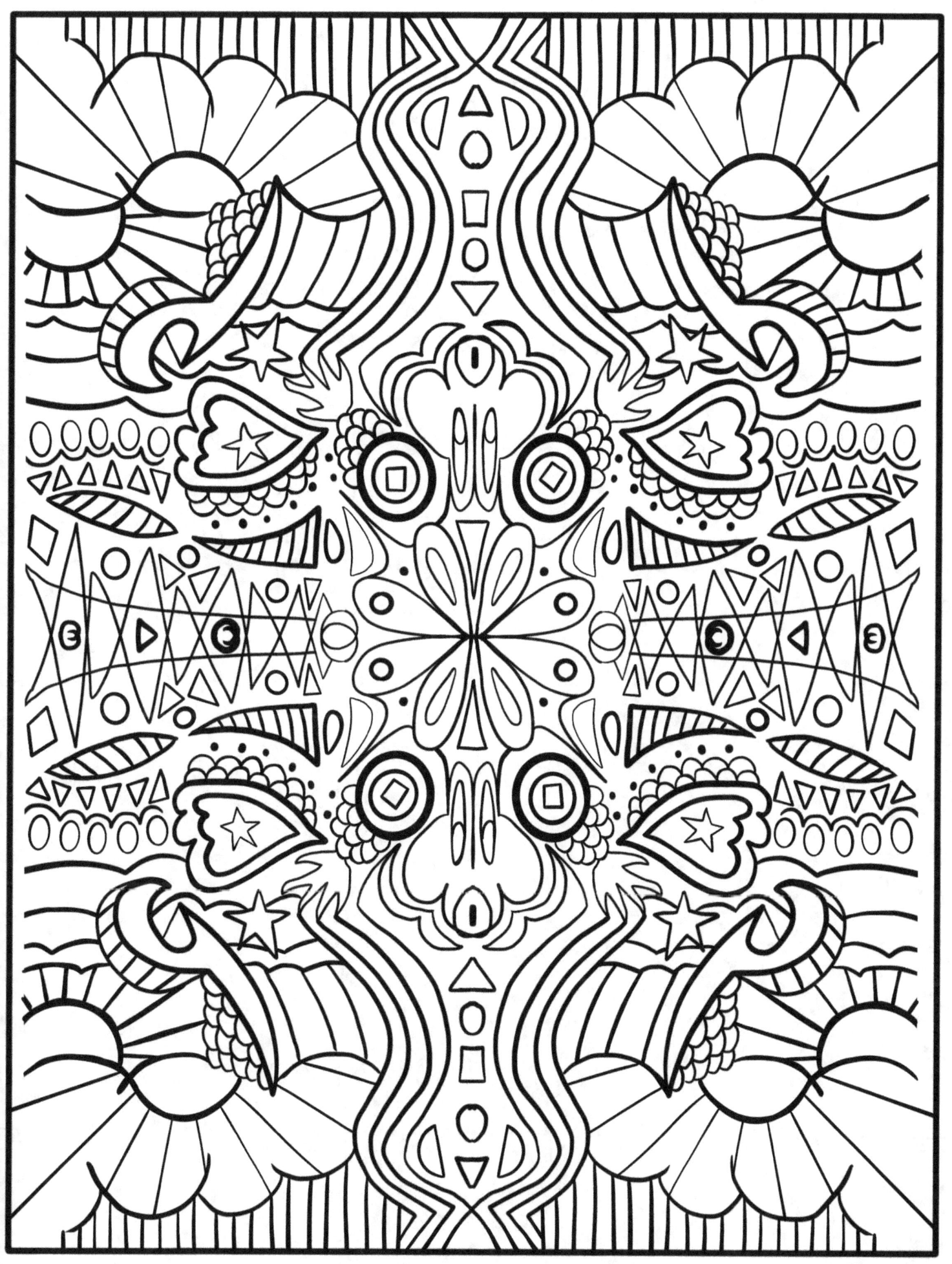

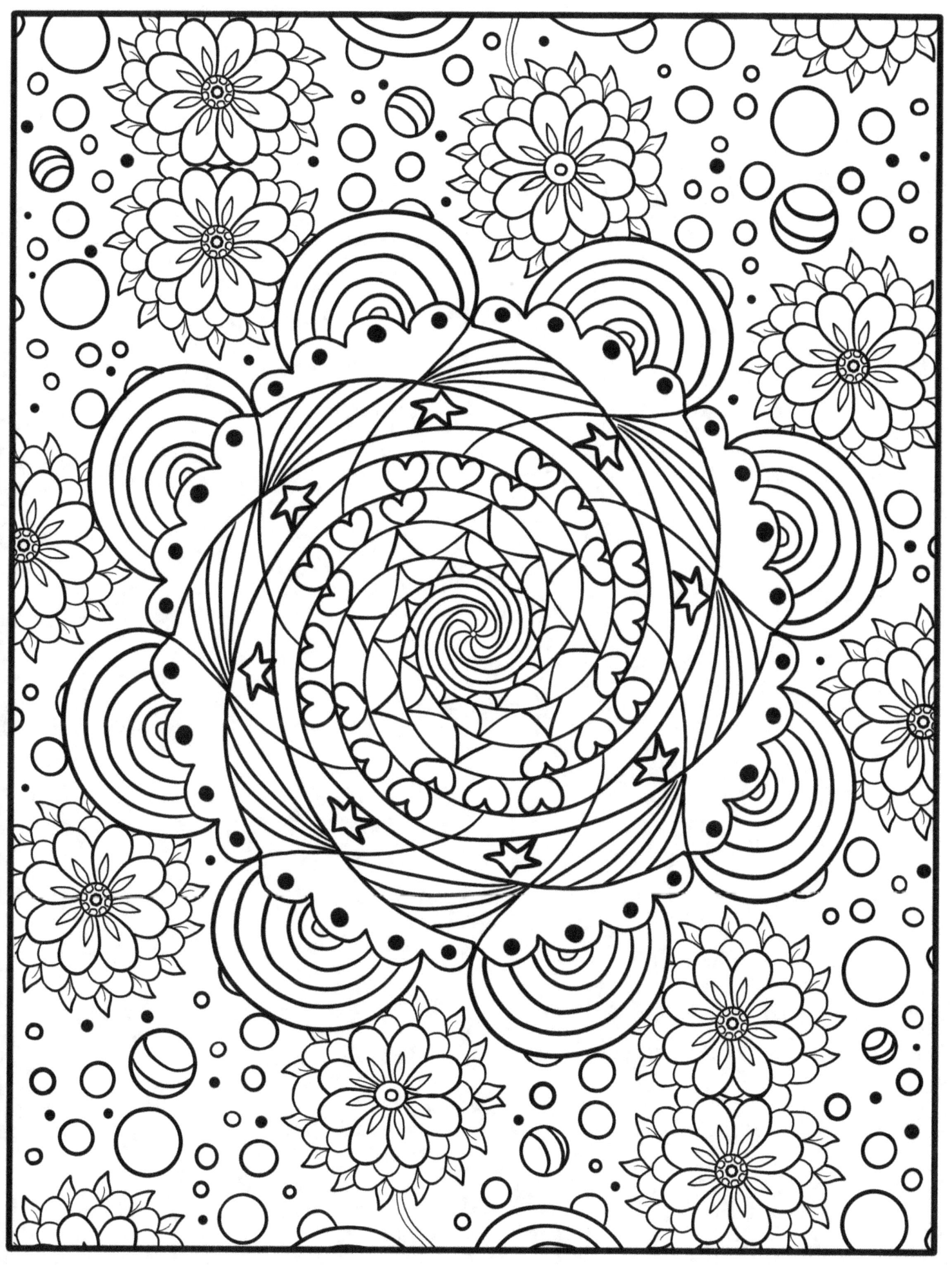

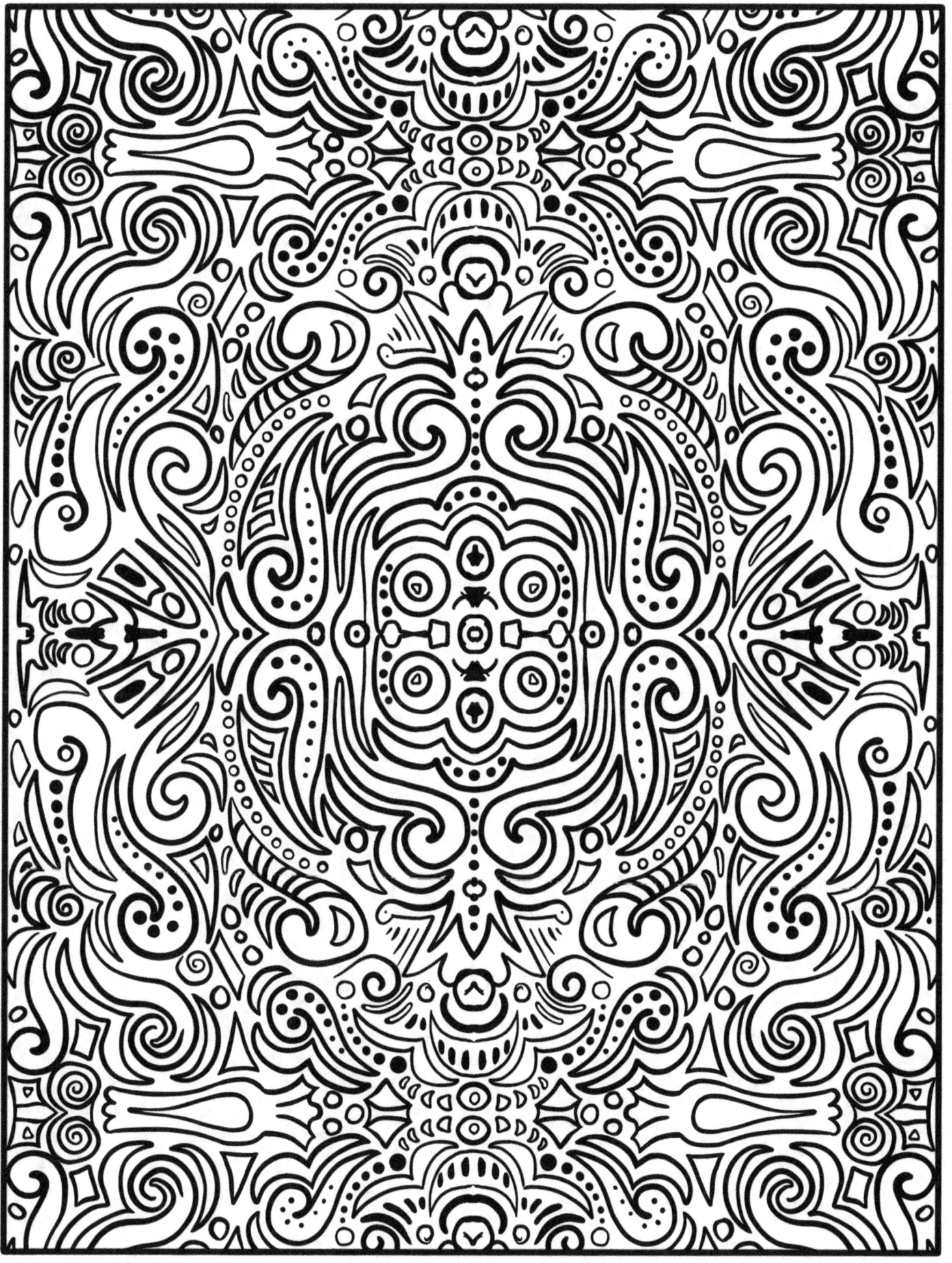

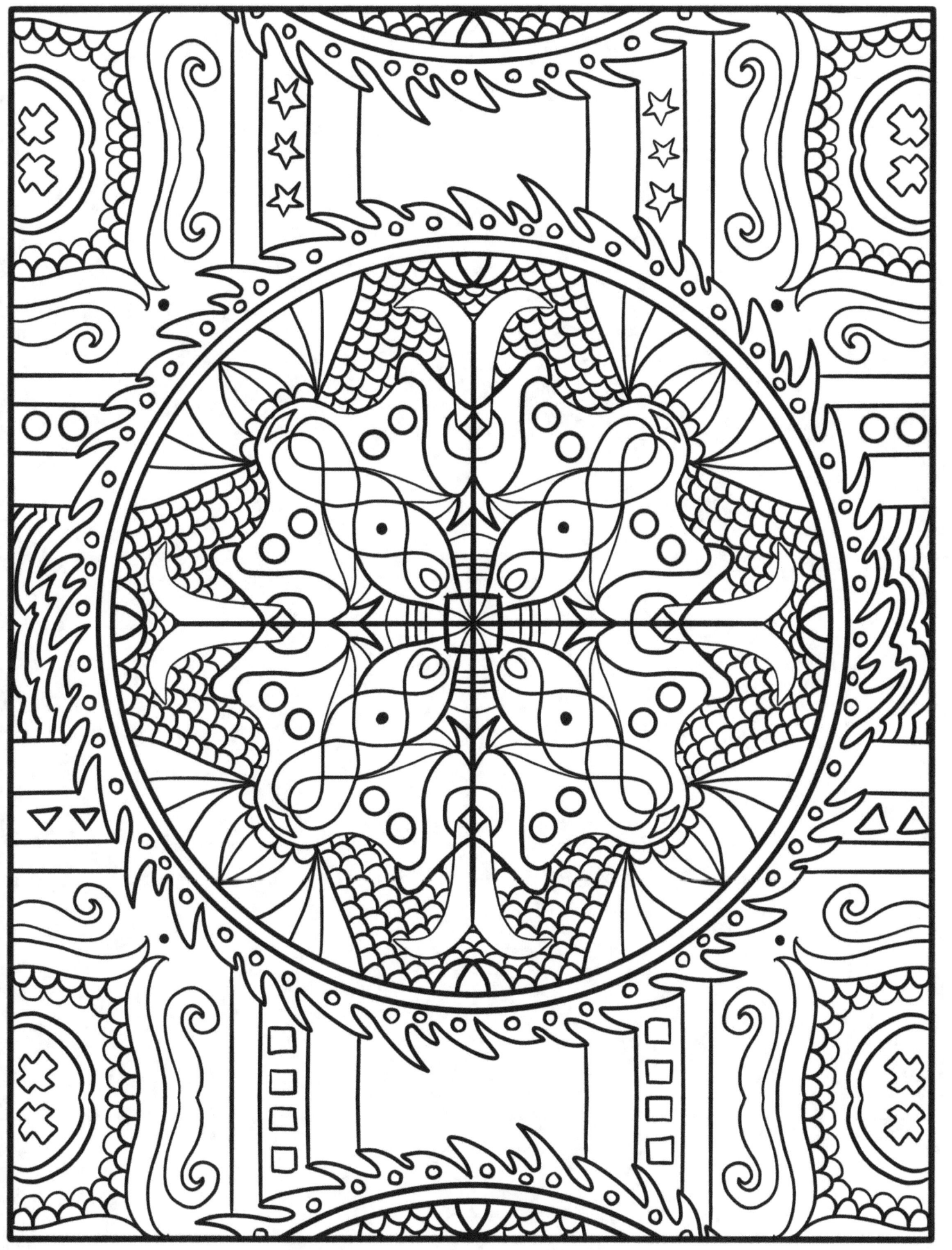

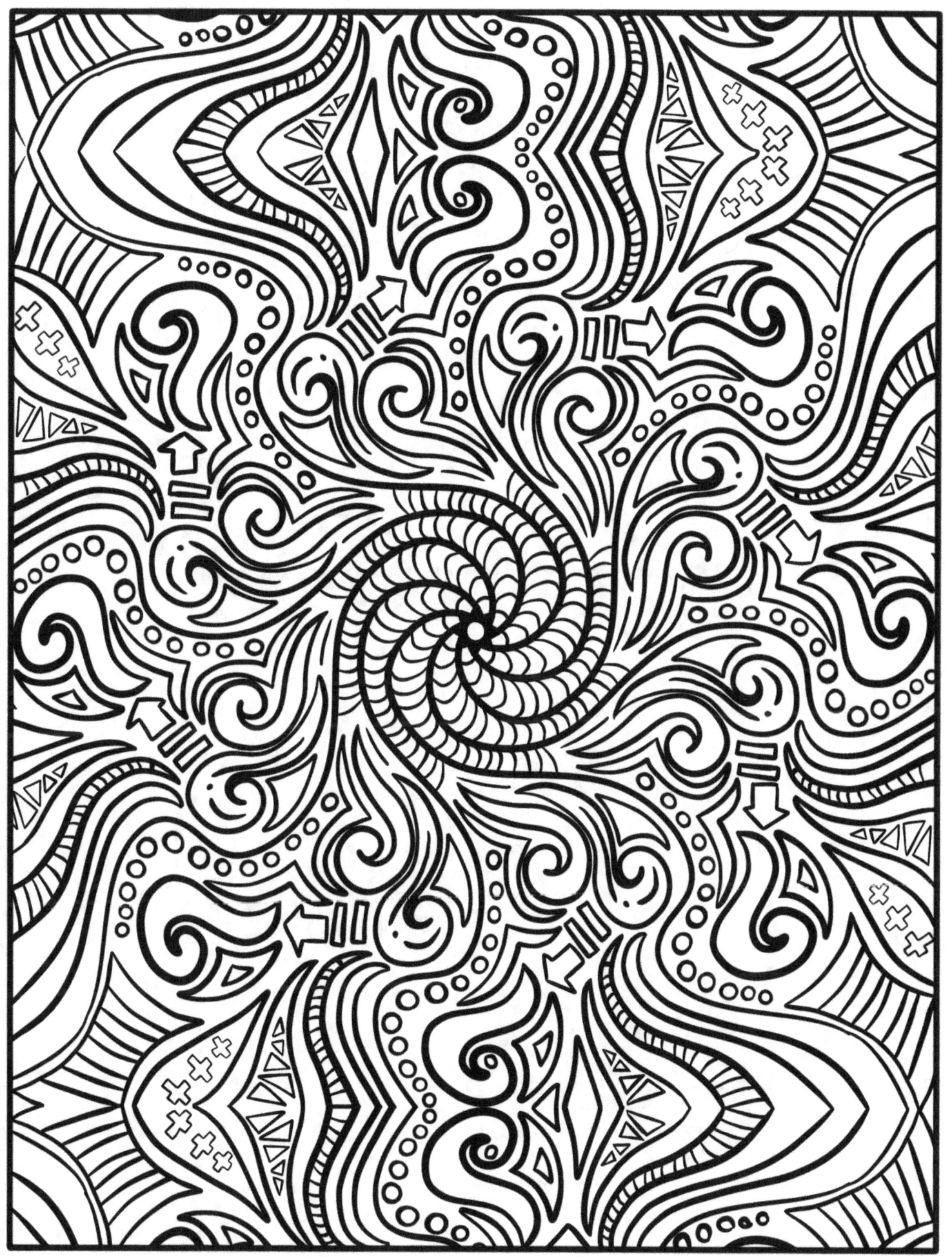

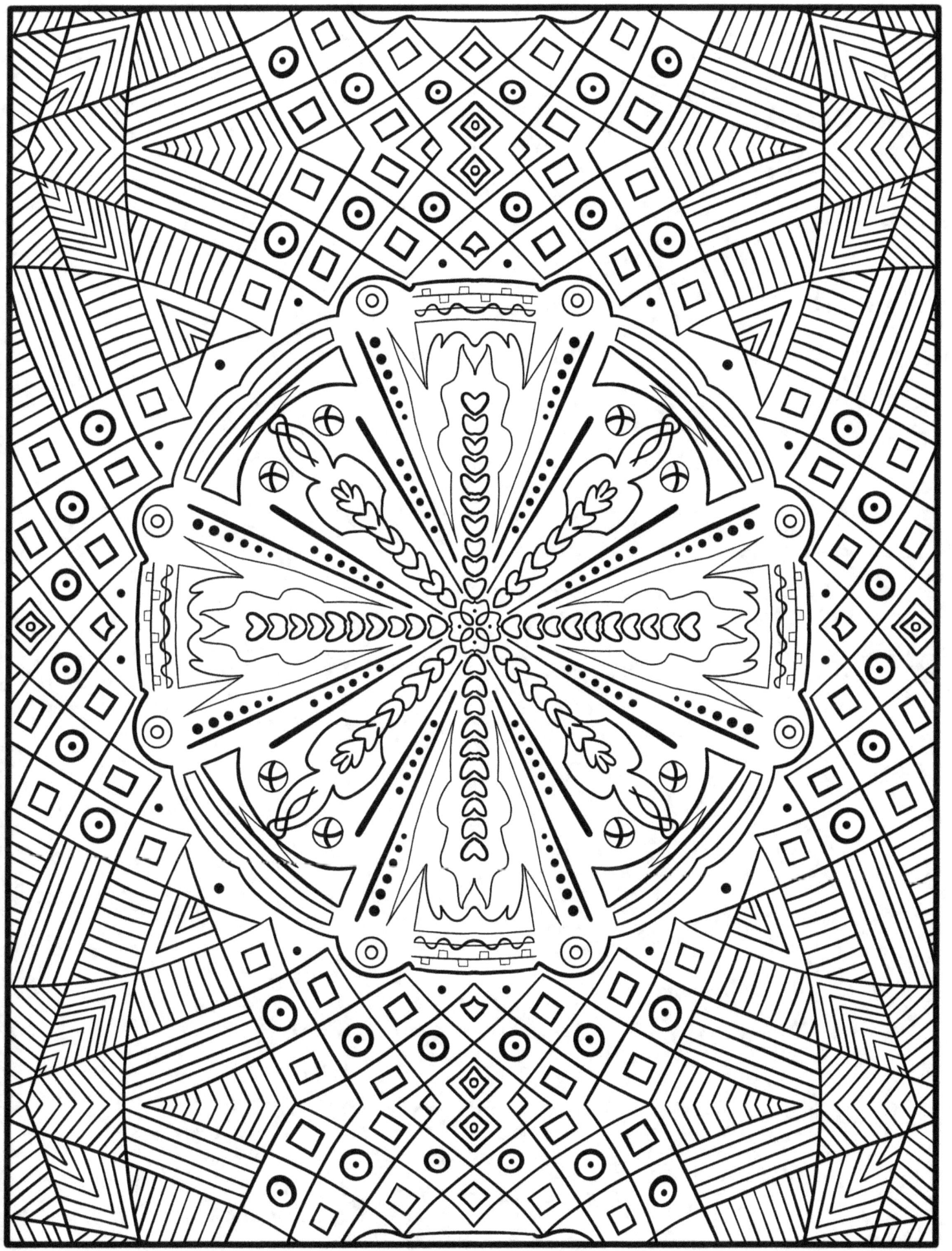

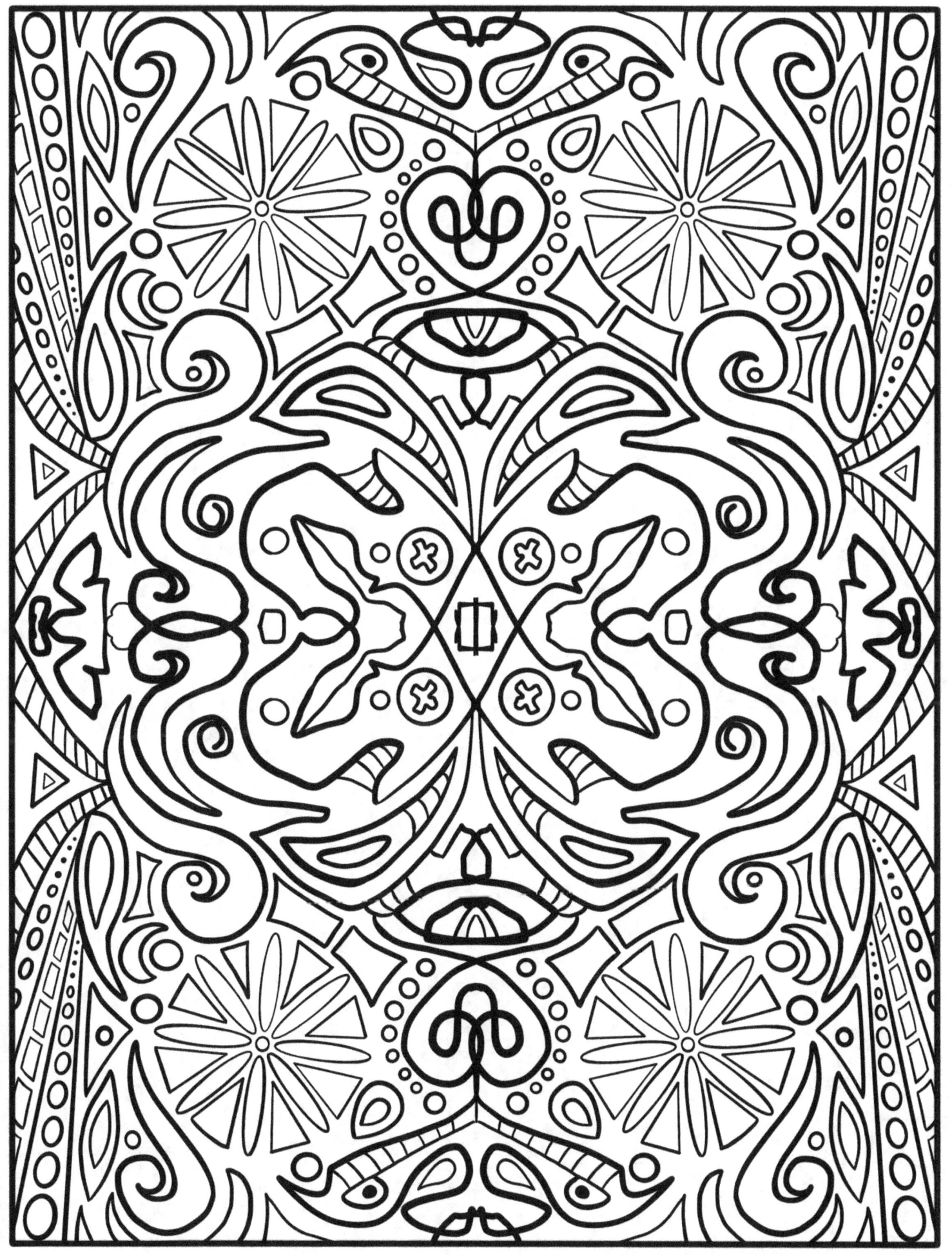

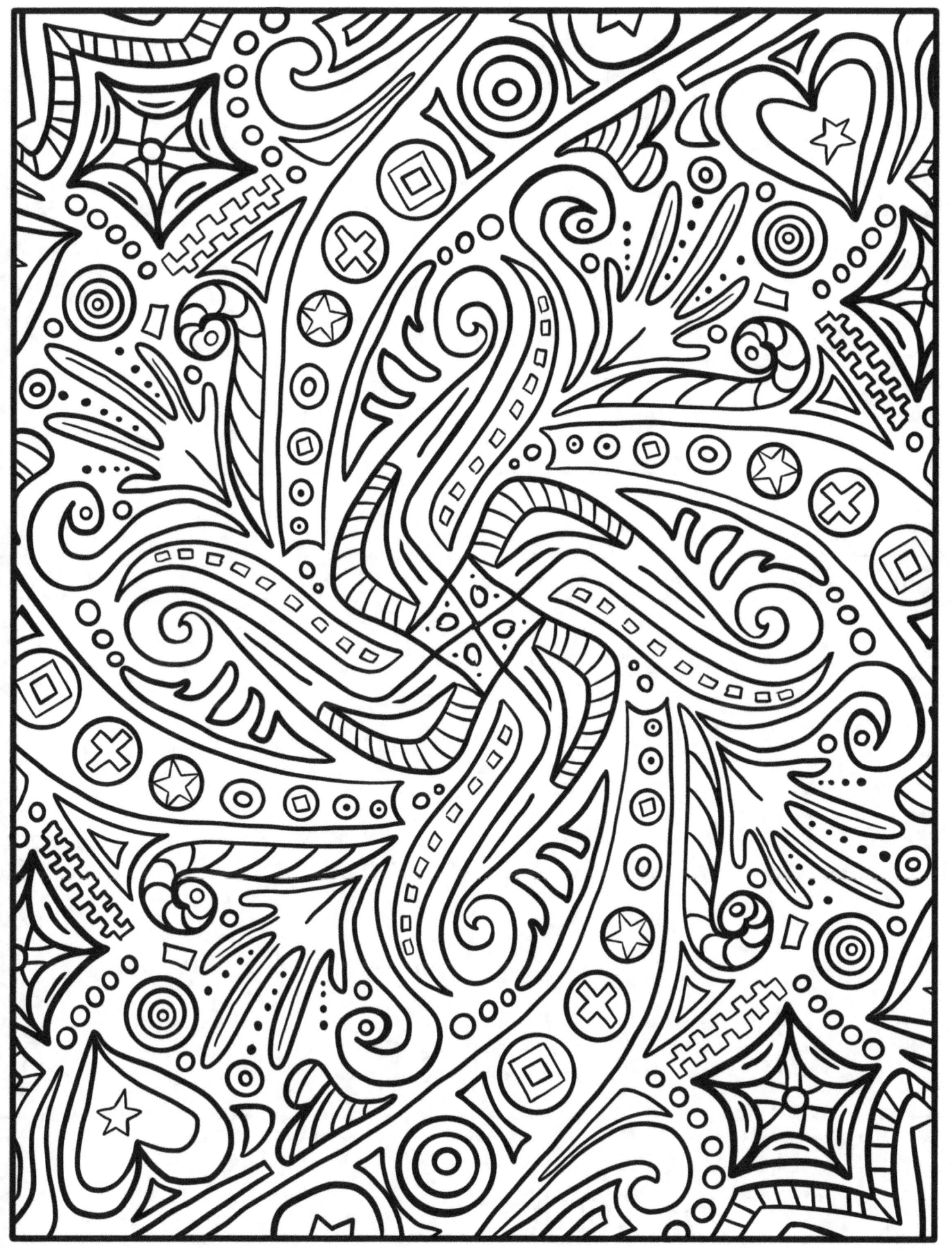

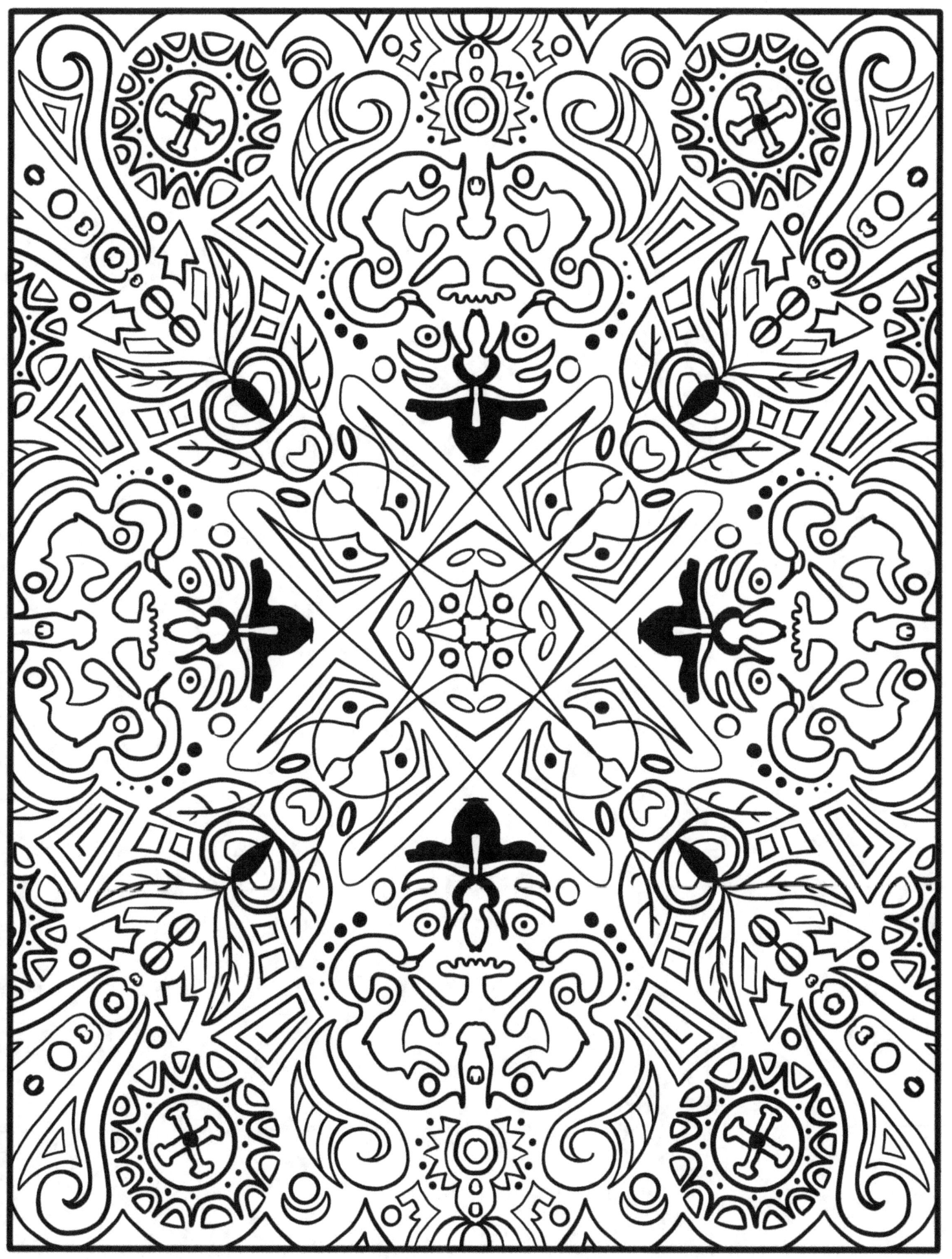

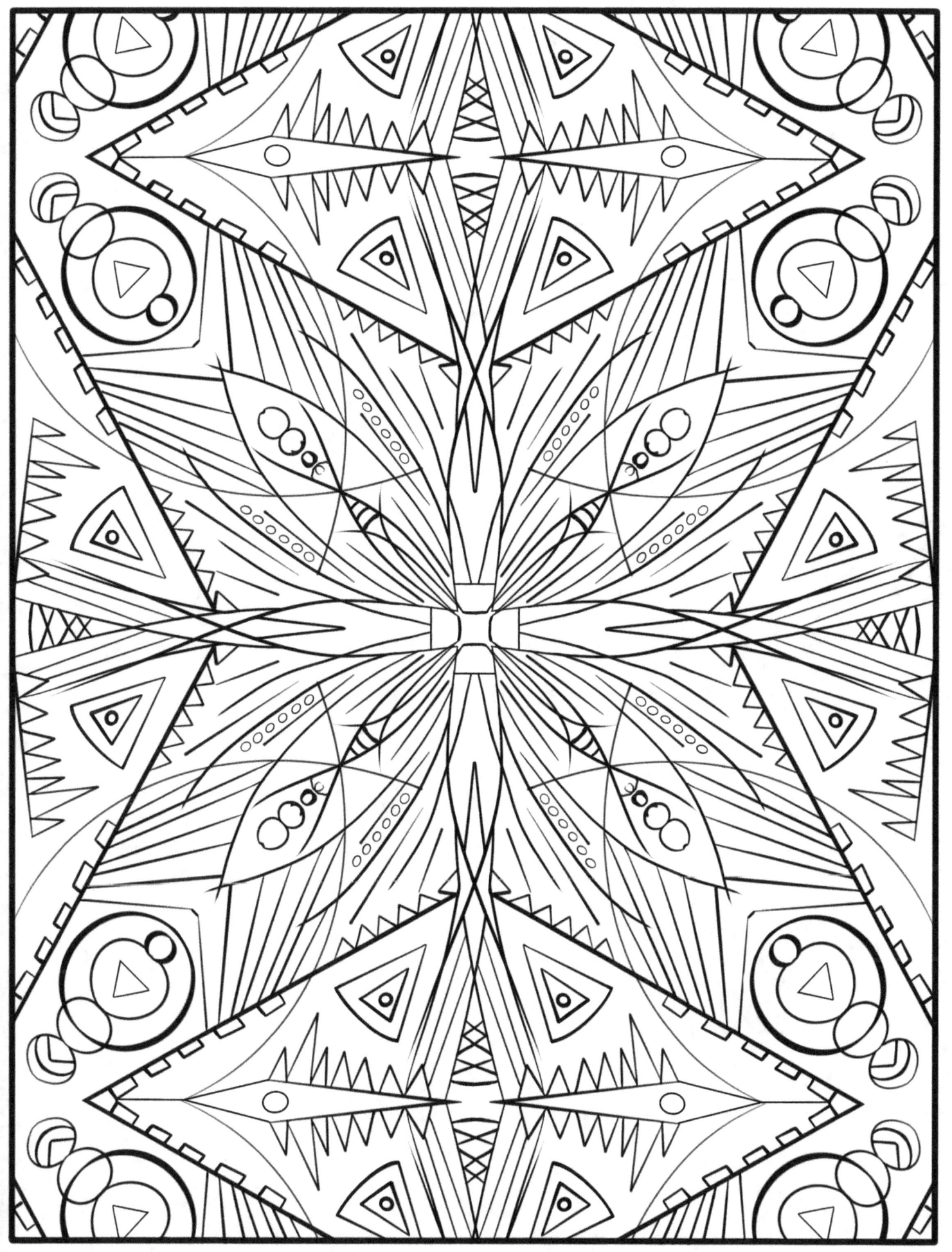

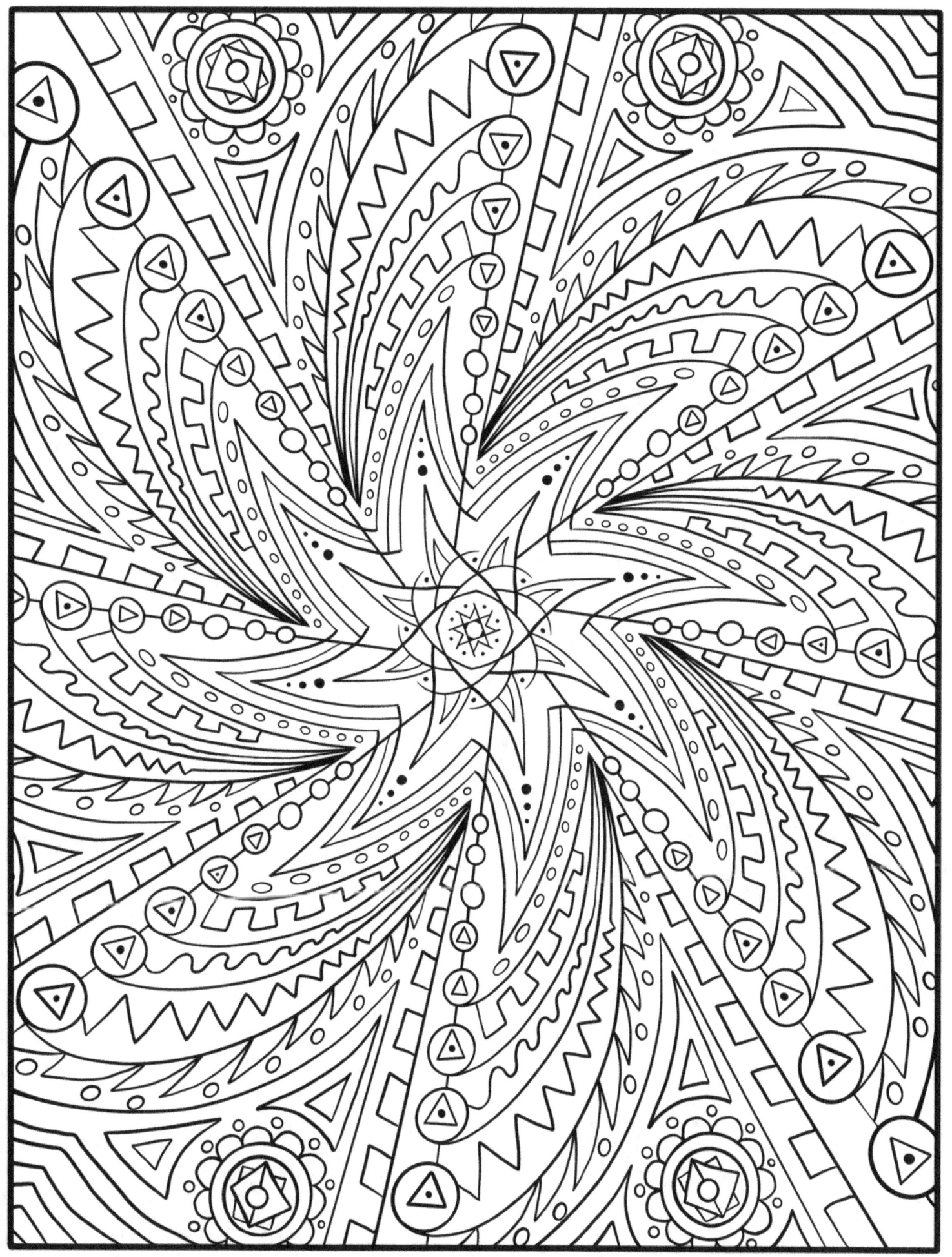

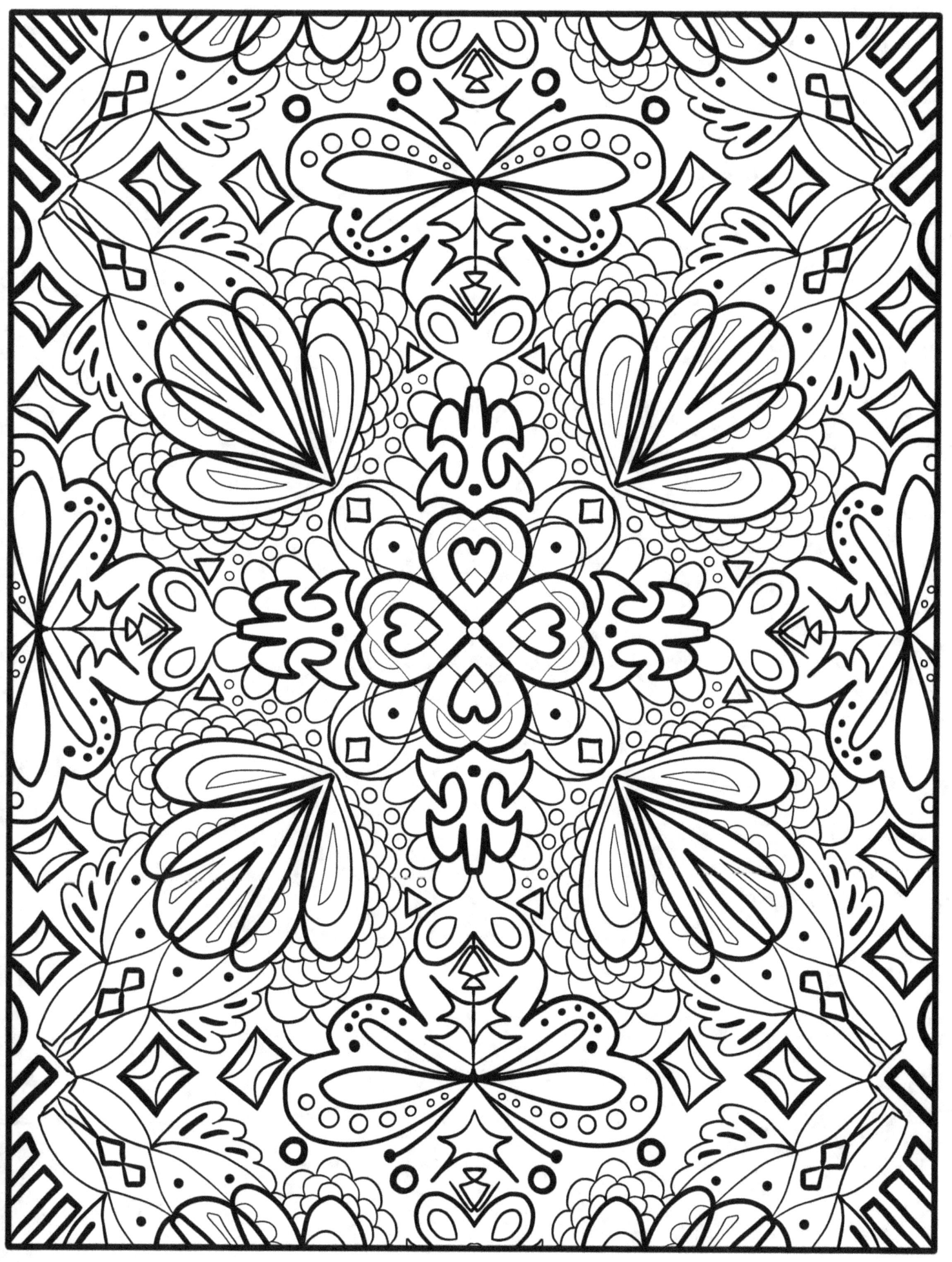

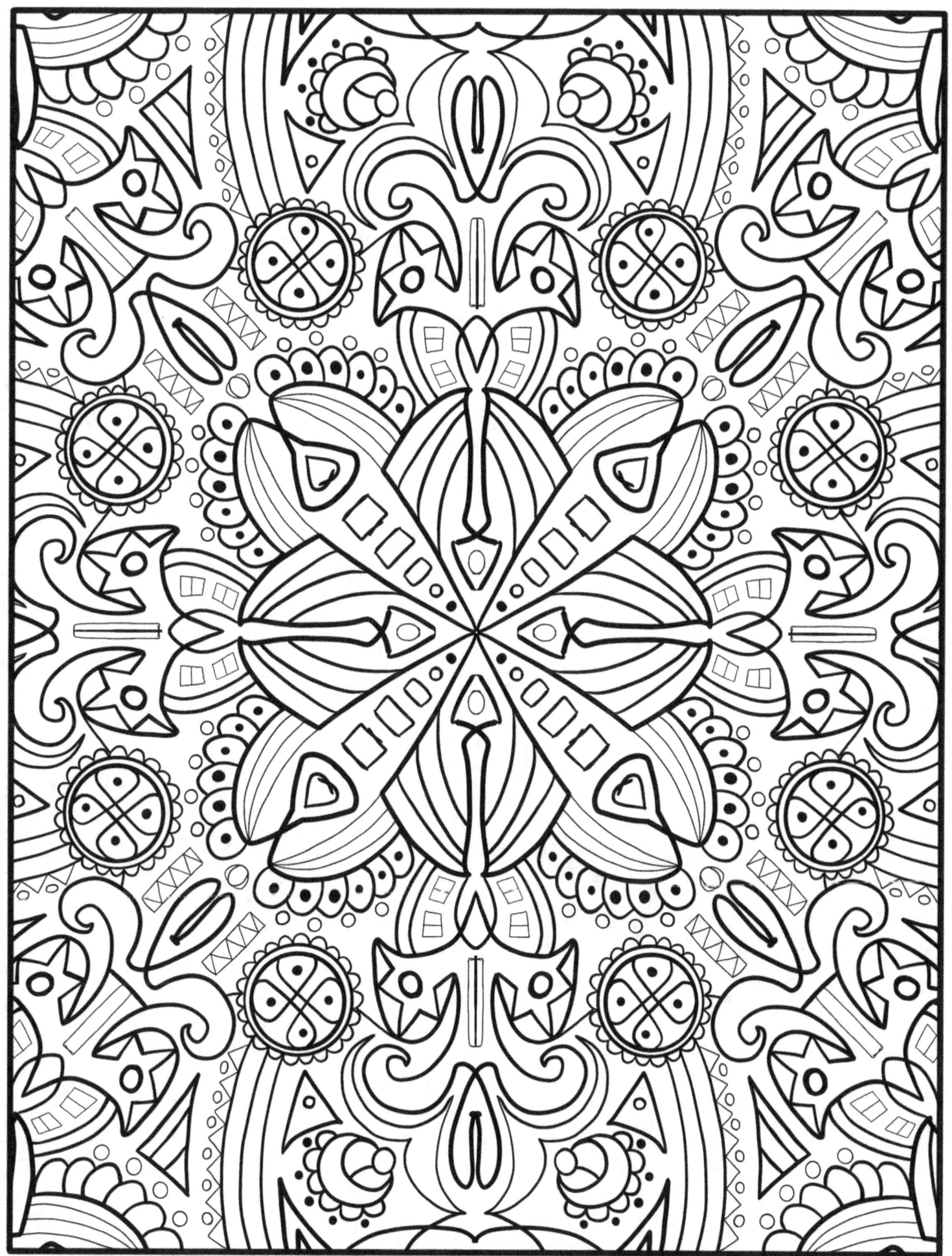

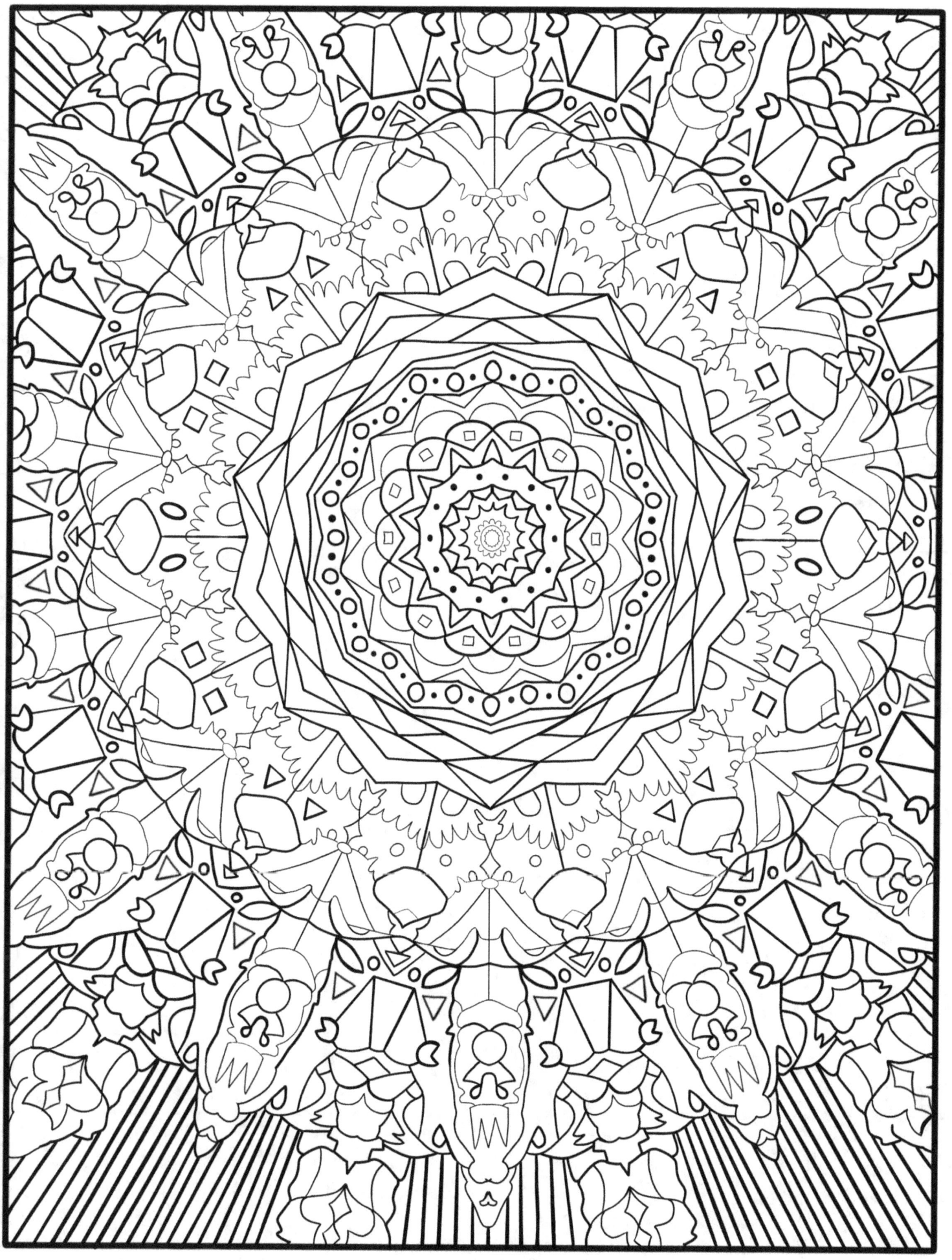

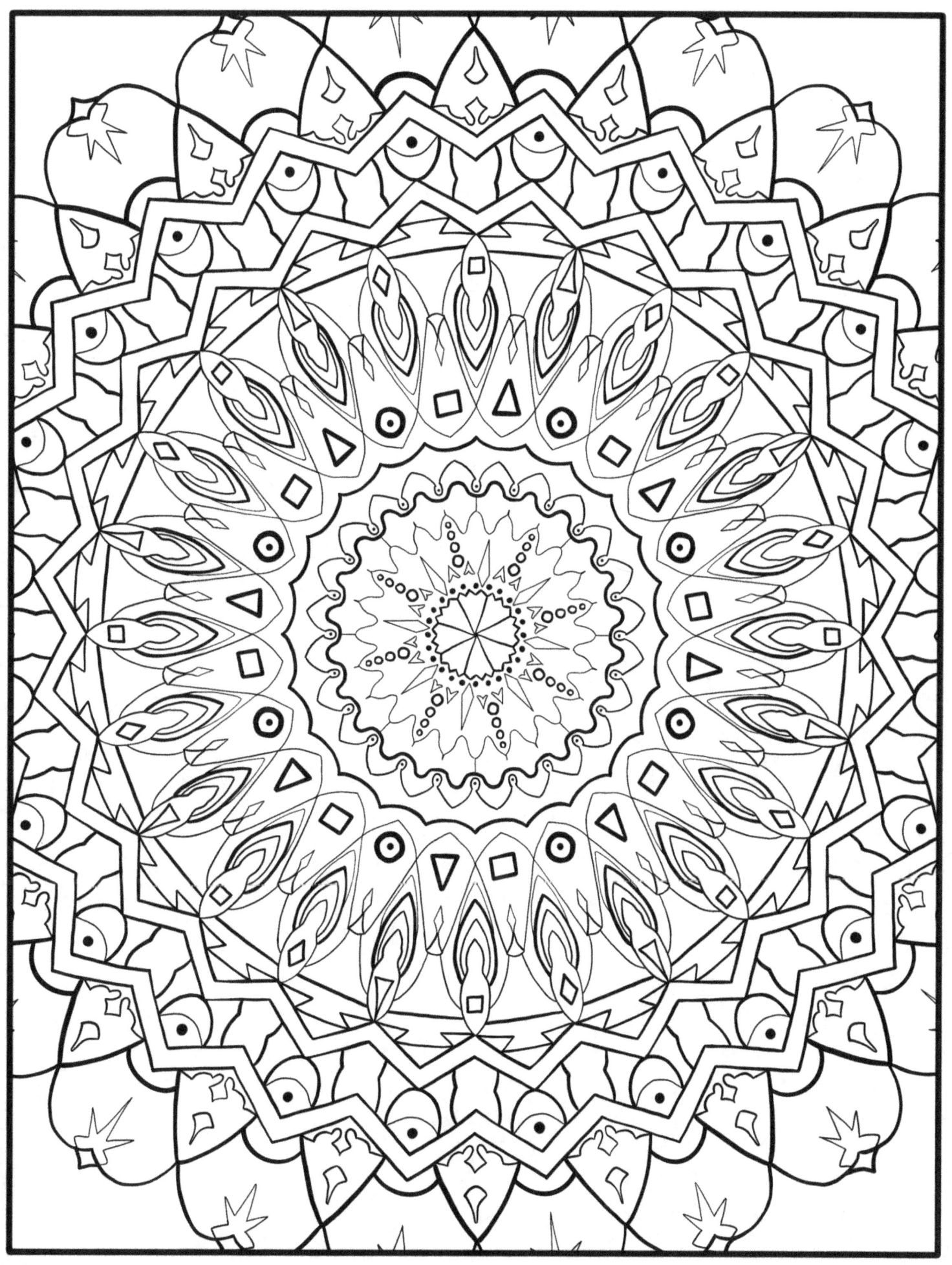

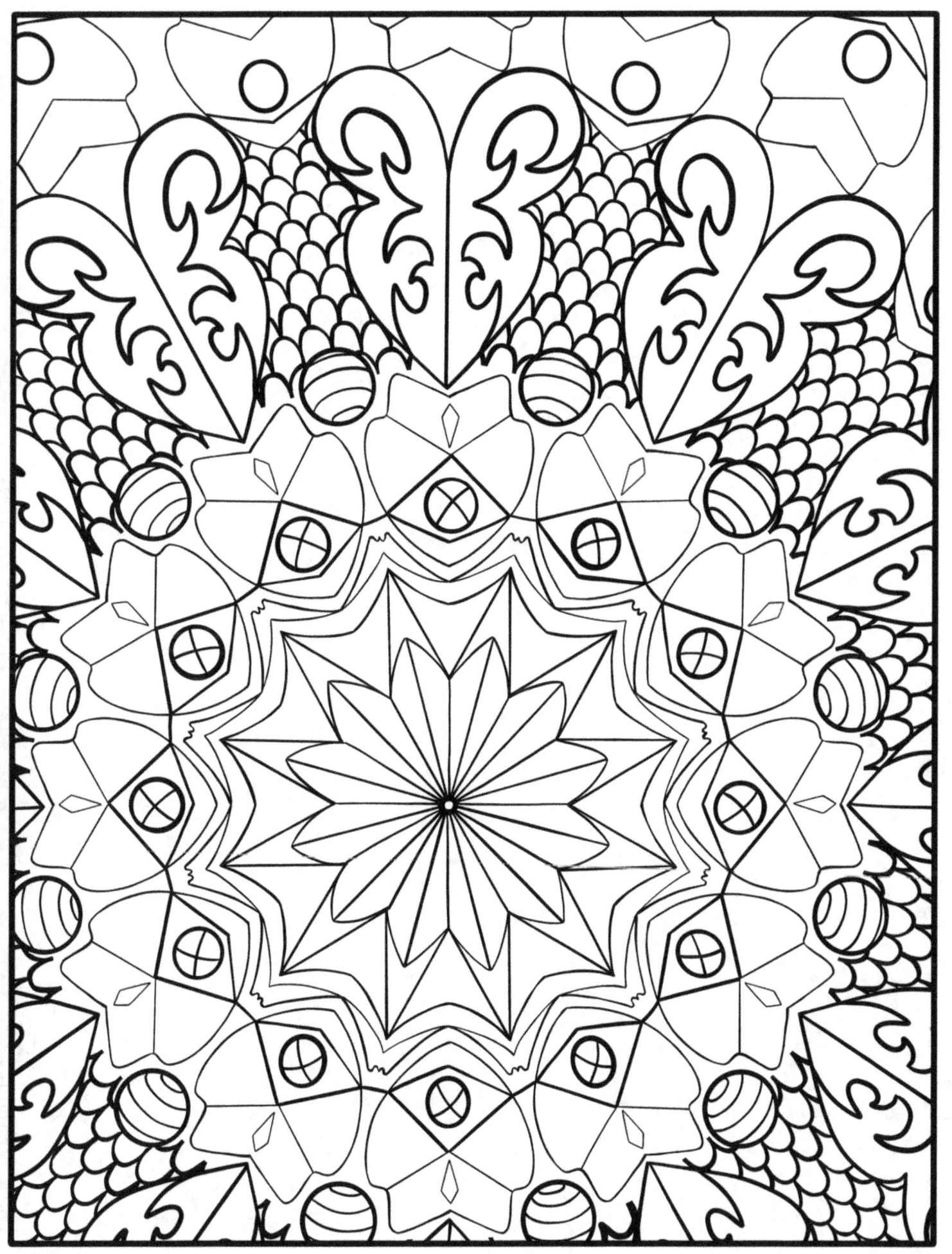

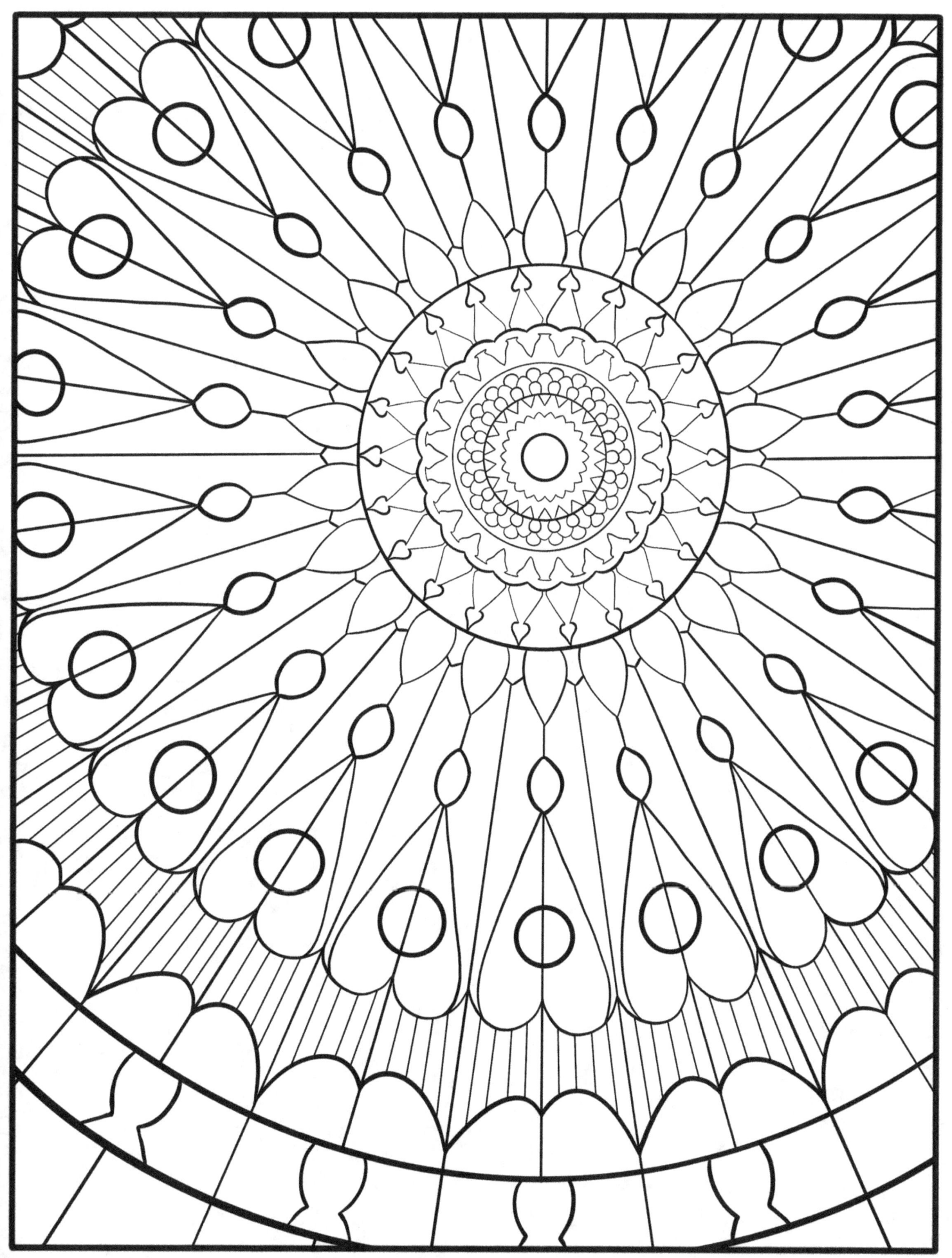

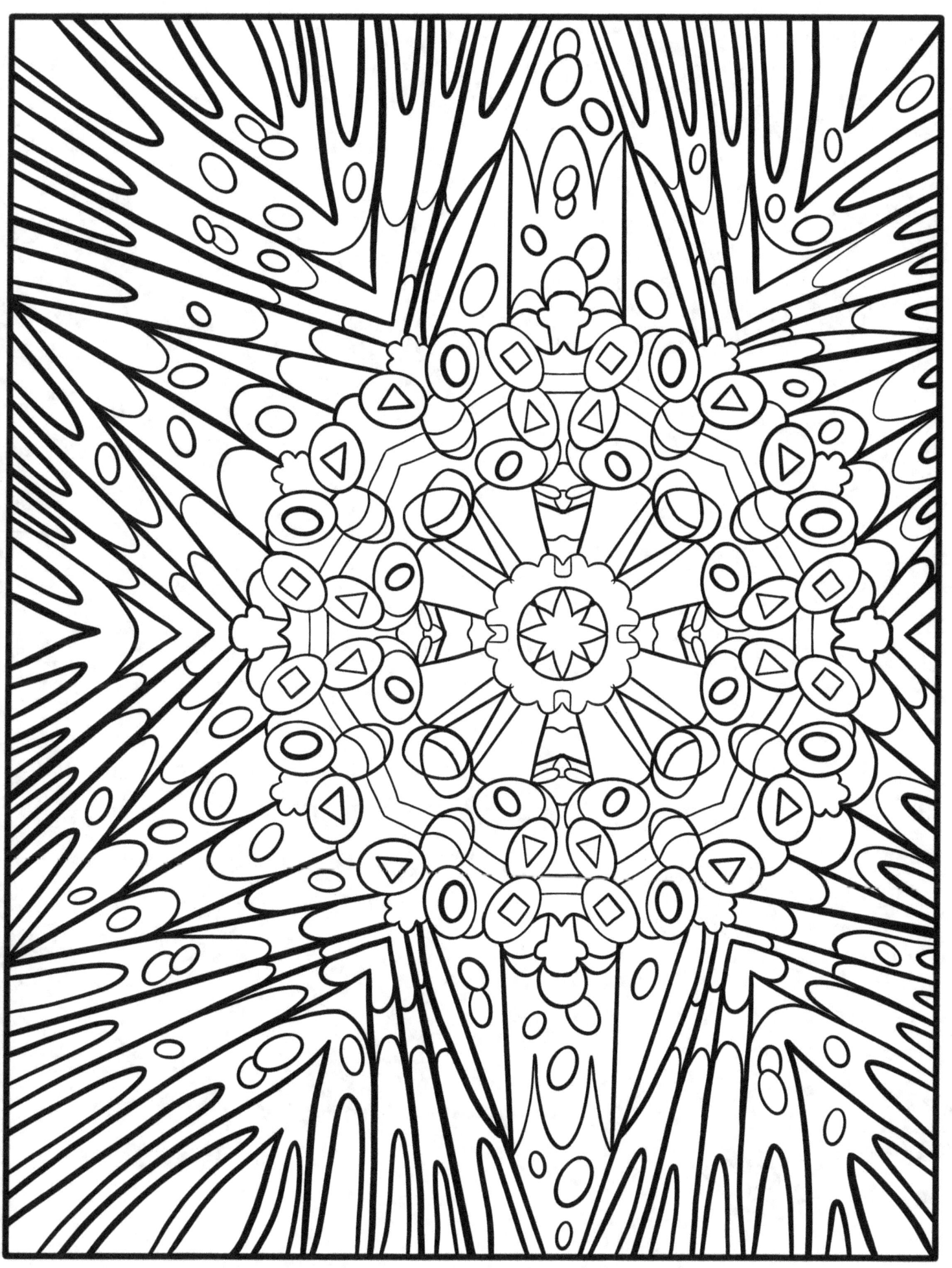

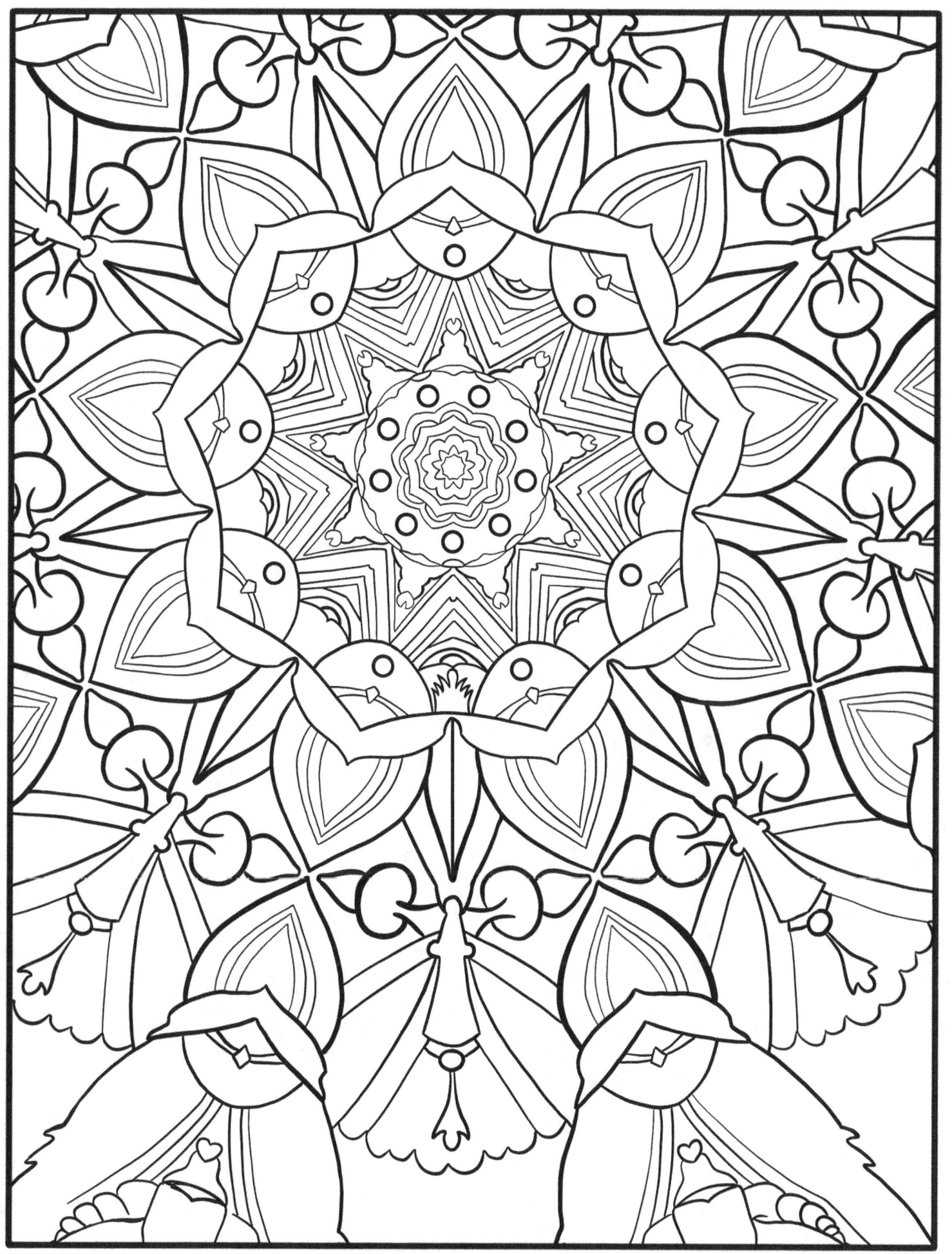

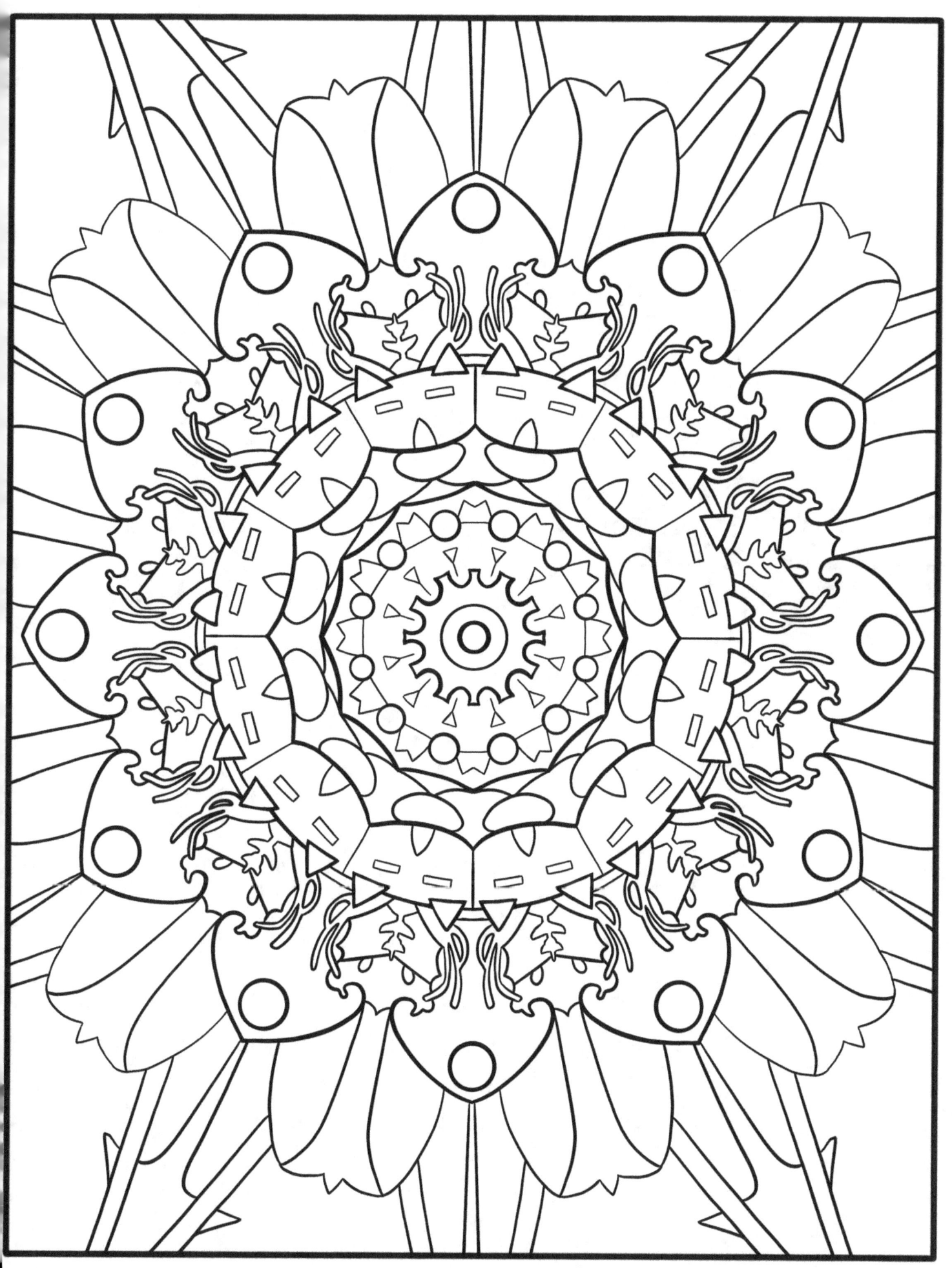

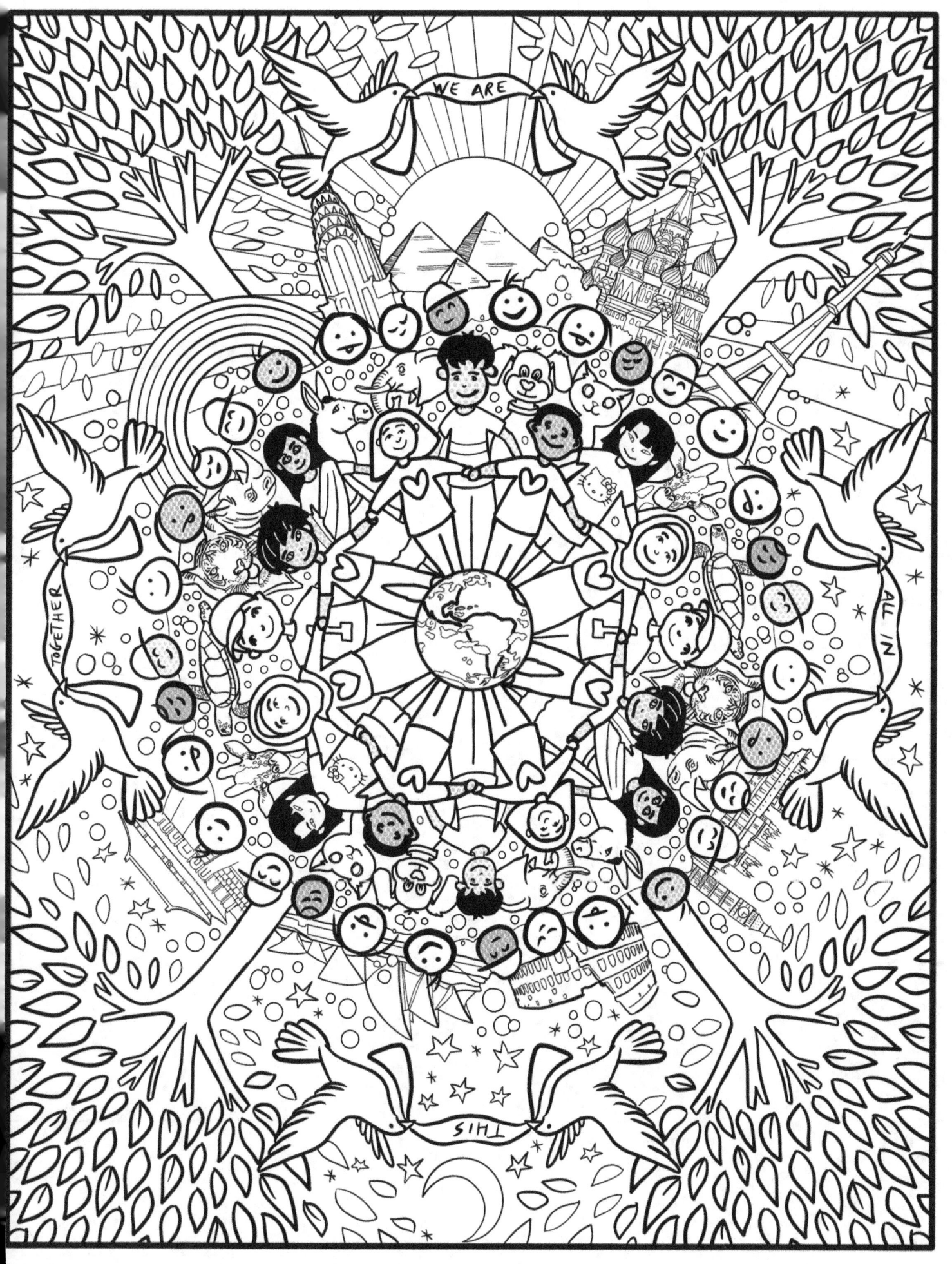

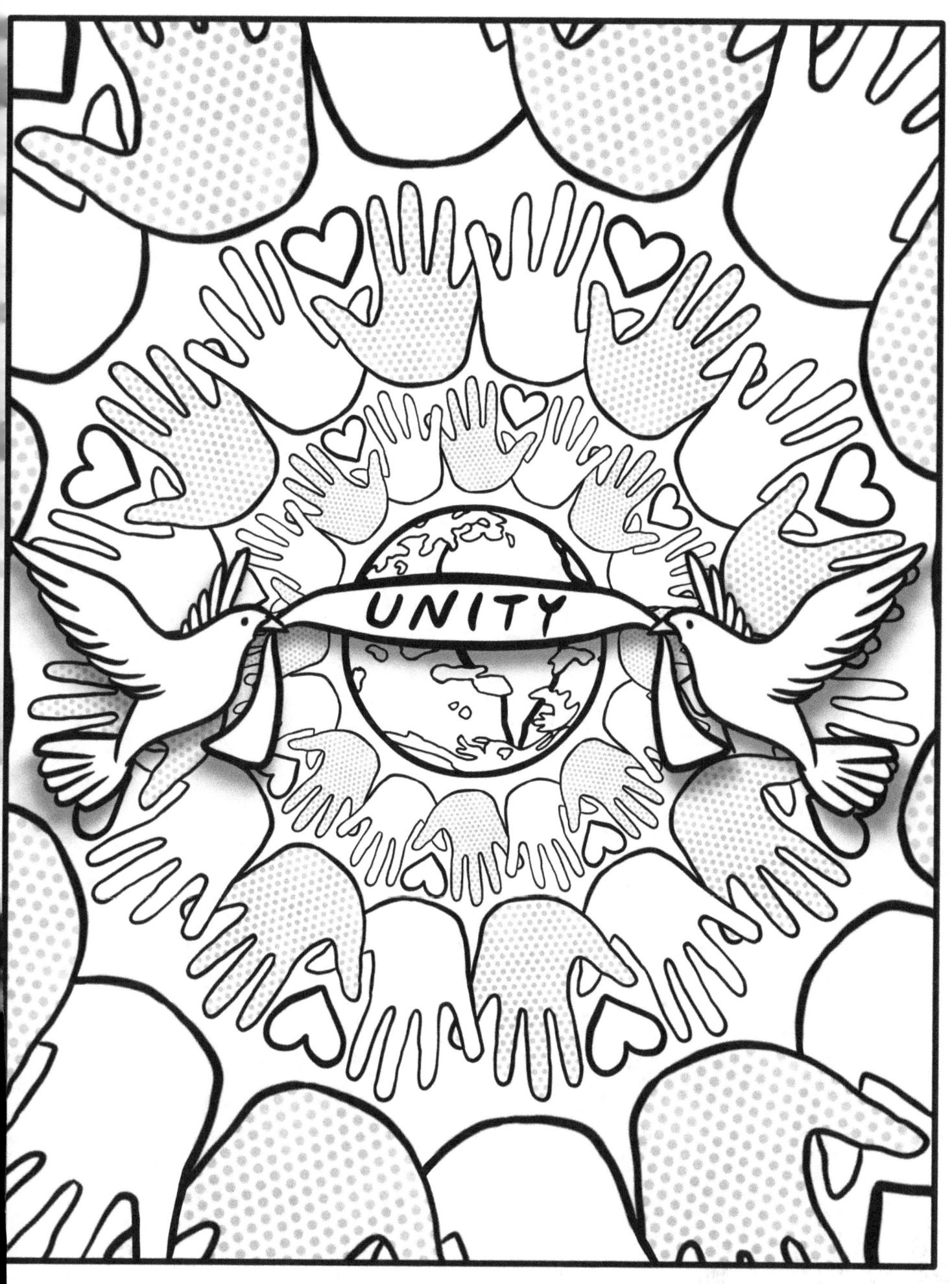